Voices

FROM THE FIELDS

Voices

FROM THE FIELDS

A BOOK OF COUNTRY SONGS
BY FARMING PEOPLE

EDITED BY RUSSELL LORD
WITH AN INTRODUCTION
BY CARL VAN DOREN

Granger Index Reprint Series

BOOKS FOR LIBRARIES PRESS
FREEPORT, NEW YORK

STANDARD BOOK NUMBER:
8369-6026-2

LIBRARY OF CONGRESS CATALOG CARD NUMBER:
78-76945

MANUFACTURED
BY
HALLMARK LITHOGRAPHERS, INC.
IN THE U.S.A.

Contents

Introduction

IF YOU study a poem down to its last elusive essence you come to what is still a mystery. Nobody knows — at least nobody has been able to tell — the difference between a perfect poem and a poem that barely misses perfection. The difference seems to be, somehow, a matter of magic, beyond reason or definition. Only taste can distinguish, and there are many tastes of various degrees of sensitiveness or maturity. When young or uncertain poets or lovers of poetry ask me about such things I usually suggest that they try their taste on *A Shropshire Lad*, reading it intently line by line and noting how hard it would be to change even a syllable without damage. For instance, so simple a line as 'White in the moon the long road lies.' Rearrange these same words so that they stand 'The long road lies white in the moon' or 'In the moon the long road lies white' or 'White lies the long road in the moon' and they have lost their delicate magic, or part of it. That magic is of course the mystery.

But the common ways of poets and poetry are not particularly mysterious. We all use words and more or less live by them. Often we cannot find the words for what we mean and would like to say. Sometimes in such cases we fall back on familiar sayings we remember. This is what proverbs — 'one man's wit and all men's wisdom' — are for: to supply to the many people who may have a given thought the happiest expression of it that has ever occurred to anybody. When we fall back on proverbs, which are usually prose, we have been thinking prose thoughts.

Sometimes we feel emotions that seem to heat our minds and call for some kind of heightened language. Generally this impulse does not go much beyond oratory. We want to make the eloquent speeches which we think would do justice to our emotions. If we cannot do that, we may listen to more gifted orators, not only admiring or envying them, but actually identifying ourselves with them, so that while we are hearing we imagine we are speaking, and at the end are nearly as much relieved as if we had spoken. When our emotions demand a heightened language more subtle than oratory, then we are poets.

Everybody is a poet now or then, if only for one moment in his life. A lover wishing he had fresh, new words for the fresh, new wonder of his love; a father or mother stung or shaken by the loveliness of a child, above the reach of available words; an overdriven man or woman longing for quiet and peace and shaping inarticulate images of them; a just man seeing injustice, needing to protest against it, and feeling powerless to convince the unjust or the unconcerned; a perceptive woman aware of beauty which has been overlooked and aching to communicate the sense of it: whoever remembers and would like to recapture; whoever hopes and would like to prefigure: these are instinctive poets and they are everywhere. Emotions rise in them, looking for an outlet in words that beat with the pulse of emotion — that is, in verse. If such instinctive poets are naturally wordless they may become sullen or irritable with the pressure of feelings dammed up inside of them; or they may read the pulsing words of other poets and get a sympathetic relief. If they have a knack or talent for using words they become poets themselves. Once in a long while one of them has genius and becomes a great poet. But there is no sharp line which at any point divides the instinctive poet, warm with however brief and cloudy an emotion which he longs to express, from the poet of genius, hot with a passion which he has the art to turn into lasting words. Poetry is a natural function of mankind.

The fifty-three contributors to *Voices from the Fields* are instinctive poets who are articulate enough to have words, and metrical forms to fit them to. Being country poets, they write of country subjects. These include what all poets write about: birth, love, work, death; earth and sky and the seasons of the year; faiths, fears, hates, aspirations, despairs; men's houses, townships, counties, countries, continents, and universes; neighbors and nations; religion, politics, housekeeping; and the characters and manners of human beings. But these particular poets are farmers, or farmers' wives or children, and they deal most often with the special and local circumstances of their calling. They live in all parts of the country, and they speak of various soils, landscapes, crops, flowers, and animals. Yet there is a remarkable — I think some readers will find it a surprising — unity in what these farmer poets think and feel. They unanimously agree in a strong, clear preference for farming as against any other trade or profession. Farming is for them not merely a livelihood, but a way of life. This book is their book of days, their anthology, their map and picture of the United States without its cities.

CARL VAN DOREN

A Note on Sources

VOICES FROM THE FIELDS is a book of poems sent in during the past ten years by readers of one of America's oldest farm papers. The paper is *The Country Home Magazine*, established at Springfield, Ohio, as *Farm & Fireside* on October 1, 1877. The publishers, Messrs. Mast and Crowell, opened Volume I, Number 1, bearing that date, with a poem, 'The Husbandman,' by John Greenleaf Whittier:

> *Give fools their gold and knaves their power,*
> *Let fortune's bubbles rise and fall,*
> *Who sows a field or tends a flower,*
> *Or plants a tree is more than all . . .*

It was a clipped piece posed as a model. Old *F & F* had neither the means nor intent to support professionals. In early issues the editors had much to say about the value of literary composition as an aid to clear thinking and character development, and wherever space could be cleared for a line of filler, 'READER, Write for the *Farm & Fireside*,' they begged.

Letters and poems still come from subscribers who heard entire issues read aloud by firelight after Bible reading, who reread them as primitive insulation on the walls of frontier cabins, and whose first and only public offering in the world of letters blossomed in that gray type. As the western march progressed, the magazine grew fatter with reader-writing. More immediately, it fattened on farm machinery advertising, for the clack of the reaper and the exactions of a commercial discipline had overtaken the primitive agriculture of the frontier. The files show time and again how pioneers overtaken by inter-dependence embrace their fate in prose, but continue to push on 'back of yonder' in song and rime.

As TIMES CHANGED farm papers changed, though never without a certain lag and reluctance. The plain gray dress beloved by print-hungry frontier families was folded away. Tentatively and awkwardly, old *F & F* experimented with make-up. About twenty years ago, when Herbert Quick was editor, the editorial shop was removed from Springfield, Ohio, to New York City, where there are experts. There in 1930 the old paper went through a face-lifting and general rejuvenation, and took its present name. From presses still in Springfield *The Country Home Magazine* goes monthly in a bright garb, downright stylish, to a million and a half or so R.F.D. boxes in all the States, but still is old-fashioned enough to have no traffic with city newsstands.

Getting out a paper for farmers has remained a remarkably personal business through the years of change. Natural-born country journalism, whether local or national, still keeps pretty generally the tone of a correspondence between individuals. The Forum, from which most of the songs in this book are reprinted, is the outgrowth of a department called 'Our Letters to Each Other,' written by a kind and gifted man, George Martin, the last and greatest of the editors under the magazine's old name and format. To see George with his cocked slouch hat and walking stick strolling down Park Avenue toward the Players' Club, you might never take him for a Nebraska countryman; but he is, with a countryman's faith in intellectual equality; and he kept alive on Park Avenue a sturdy and honorable tradition of personal journalism. 'Write up to them, and they'll write up to you,' he would tell us. 'Just because you're in the business of being articulate, don't think you're God Almighty on a cloud.' Wheeler McMillen, the present Editor, who broke in on the staff about the same time I did, in the early nineteen-twenties, dedicated his first book, *Too Many Farmers:* 'To George Martin: For Very Good Reasons.'

FORUM & AG'IN EM, we called the department when it started in August, 1927. When the pun grew old we shortened the title. First as a staff associate in New York, and now as a contributing editor on a small place of my own, I have been running The Forum ever since it started. My feeling about the material, about many of the writers, and about the magazine which has given them voice, is personal, even intimate; so there is no use in my pretending to be altogether objective, or in trying to write that way.

The Forum is not a poetry column but a printed meeting of country people, with anywhere from twenty to seventy different voices, month by month. Usually there is room for only one poem a month, an opening song, printed in the poet's place, at the top. At first the department gave no space to song, and little to harmony of any sort. It was a noisy letter column, with highly personal discussions — about farm relief, religion, overworked wives, smoking, drinking, dancing, infidelity, birth control, crop control, one-piece bathing suits, divorce, tractors, corporal punishment, etc., describing somewhat meaningless cycles of diminishing velocity, as letter-column discussions will. The thing began to turn on itself and run down. Our pages had always been open to poets and harmonizers, and in 1931 we threw ourselves wide open. We offered ten dollars for the best poem written by anyone of any age who had never before submitted verse to an editor, with this remark:

'Maiden teachers who squirm their eyes and intone when reading have aroused in the American male, particularly, the crippling conviction that to sing with a pencil is affected and queer. Nonsense. The A.E.F. wrote more and better verse per capita than any literary society you could name. To our way of thinking, people ought to write verse, good and bad, with as little shame and self-consciousness as they feel when singing in the bath-tub or when riding at a gallop or when swinging down a mountainside at sixty.'

Trying to figure how many rimed offerings we must have read in manuscript since then, I am sure that it has come to no less than twenty thousand. This book contains most of the published ones and others held for years in hope of room enough to print them.

BEN H. SMITH, who has more pieces here than anyone else, sends in as many as eighty at a time. He is a grower of strawberry plants in southern Illinois. Between growing seasons he makes a little extra money typing and criticizing the work of other poets at twenty-five cents apiece, by occasional sales of his own work, and by playing the banjo at Holy Roller meetings in the hills. Since 1936 he has been writing, gratis, for the nearby weekly *Jonesboro Gazette*, a column called 'Where the Hills Slope Upward.'

'My Own Land,' the first poem in the book, was written about Nebraska, apparently his birthplace, by Herbert

Everell Rittenburg, a hired man in Virginia, tormented by homelessness, poverty and illness.

> *Is there no song that I may sing?*
> *Waits there no perfect song for me...?*

I have added brief notes about him, and about other major contributors, grouping such comment with their work.

Few of the authors here brought together are men and women torn by want or rootless. They are substantial people, reasonably happy, busy tending the earth, teaching school, keeping house and rearing families. Some are grandparents, taking it easier now; some are youngsters; but most of them are farmwives and farmers of the middle years, with families still on their hands; wives and husbands pushed and steadied through days of hard work by a sense of guardianship over living things, and by the responsibilities of property.

A man plowing, a woman doing housework, may find time to think and get at meanings, but when it comes to putting them down on paper, the time is usually short — an hour or so between dark and dawn. Most of these songs are short. They go to the point in straight declarative sentences, and they sound a clear note:

> There shall be songs when I have tired of singing
>   Of love and pain...

> ... Then softly fell the evening of content...

> But overhead the same deep sky still burned
>   By day; and all the lifted lamps of night
> Flared welcome...

> The near earth rears them: mothers with deep breasts...
>   Their days are long and hard. They are content
> If they can serve the common ways of men.

When we dug her narrow bed,
Buds were slowly waking...

                                        ...The clean
And tender resurrection of the spring.

A poet, as I understand it, is one who can strike with
words through the externals of our whirling existence, and
proclaim meanings that endure. Surely, the writing busi-
ness cannot have all the poets.

THINGS LOOK BETTER now, and there is no point in dwell-
ing on past misery; but it should at least be noted that
farming people wrote most of these songs during the hard-
est of years for American farmers, the late nineteen-
twenties and early nineteen-thirties. Changed times
brought a changed mood, and more poetry. As *F & F's*
younger daughter, in modern dress, *The Country Home
Magazine* had been questioning, and at times assailing,
most of the assumptions of the old-time sweat-and-blood
agriculture and of the puritan-pioneer dogma. Editori-
ally, we had denounced the cherished little red school-
house as a 'breeder of ignorance' and the source of a crip-
pling educational inequality between farm and city. We
had suggested interdenominational churches and a critical
appraisal of elders meanly pious. We had discussed con-
traception, had defended cigarette advertisements with
women in them, and had turned, month after month, an
attentive ear to arguments for highly centralized corpora-
tion farming. We had described overwork as the most
dangerous form of American intemperance, and had
urged upon farm women a personal revolt against the old
patriarchal absolutism which still makes many American

farm homes, with money enough to allow a certain amount of ease and civilization, places of tyranny, littleness, and hate. We had gone so far as to assert, in this connection, that the wife should have equal access to the family purse or checking account; and that it is in no way sinful to have breakfast in bed. (Out of the breakfast-in-bed debate grew, obliquely, the verse called 'At the Funeral,' which I have brought forward to page 10 of this book.)

To all such goads and sallies the unalterable old-timers responded, naturally, with a great roar; and the tone of their communications commanded respect. It bit deep. It had a furious, pent-up, spiritual force. For all our insistence on a greater freedom, a less cramping philosophy, or religion, we still have nothing as sustaining or as unifying to offer — we younger ones.

But it was an aging and a dwindling roar. Our younger readers, speaking generally, were all for progress. Passing on to still higher concepts we were about to declare that anyone who spanks a troublesome child is a sadist, when suddenly progress went to pieces, let us all down.

EARTH IS OUR REFUGE whenever progress fails us. Almost immediately after Black Friday, 1929, in New York City the realistic farm novel lacked a market. The pastoral tone was the thing now; and around Washington Square, which is named for a farmer, the most civilized of Americans yearned for nothing so much as a little place in the country and a few hens.

We all know that impulse. It settled this country. It is in our blood. Our every spell of panic and depression from pre-revolutionary times onward had been attended by a retreat, in person and in thought, toward the largely imagined simplicities of a pioneer or pastoral order. In the fearful days of '29 and the early 'thirties, this impulse, this almost biological yearning to re-enter the womb of time, to be absorbed in the earth's processes, and to be let alone, was deeply felt in the open country, as well as in the town.

But with a difference. Countrymen know, in good times and bad, that earth is no fond mother eager to provide for or to welcome her living children back. Earth is beautiful, and at times comforting, beyond any words that can be summoned to describe her; but she weans you when she bears you. After that, it's your struggle, none of her concern. Earth is hard. Countrymen know this; and the knowledge tempers their lyrics.

So for one reason or another The Forum as it grew older became quieter. Even the sometimes cocky Chair, as the presiding editor is called, was not so sure. More and more the discussions sought, with a common acknowledgment of distress and bewilderment, something to tie to, remember, believe.

Strangely (or naturally, according to how you look at it) the prevailing note in the communications through the darkest years — after it had ceased to be simply a farm depression — grew serene and proud. *'Give fools their gold and knaves their power'* was still the song of husbandmen struggling for gold and power enough to keep going.

Until their homes are taken, farmers are unlikely to rise and march. That is the source of their worldly weakness and long strength. In good times and bad they will talk about money matters, but to draw a response of depth and magnitude, give them chance to speak or sing of fundamental matters: of hard old Earth, our common mother and refuge; of life's eternal renewal by crops and by children; of farms that earn a living and, more than that, release from meaningless noise, triviality and display — farms that are homes.

Firesides give way to radiators. Horseflesh gives way to gas. Freehold ownership gives way to supervised tenancy and centralized management. Bill boards, hot-dog stands, and olde cabin dancehalls sprout like toadstools. Loudspeakers pour scum from the air waves along roads once safe, removed, and peaceful. But you can move back from the main roads and away from the radio. The fields are still there, with the wind and sun upon them. They offer a comparative security, and a healing solitude. And those who tend the fields (so farmers believe and sing) gain ownerless possessions and compensations which no city person, however great or rich, can claim.

RUSSELL LORD

'THORN MEADOW'
HARFORD COUNTY, MARYLAND
May, 1937

I   *OPENING SONGS*

My Own Land

I have come back at last to my own land
    And found the sweet, wild grass torn
        quite away
From round the old sod house that used to
        stand
    Upon the prairie's wide expanse of gray.
The house that knew my childhood's grief
        and mirth,
    The well-remembered house where I was
        born,
Had crumpled to a grave-like mound of
        earth
    I scarce could find among the tall green
        corn.

But overhead the same deep sky still burned
    By day; and all the lifted lamps of night
Flared welcome to a prodigal returned
    To seek, among the shards of youth, the
        light
That lured him forth upon his first high
        quest;
And now, please God, may guide him home
        to rest.

Herbert Everell Rittenburg, Virginia

Song

Last night the seeking wind sang in the
    shadow
  Its old sweet song of bud and blossom rife.
Today the birds are singing in the meadow
  And in the lane the tulips wake to life.

By orchards where of old we used to wander
  And watch the Aprils slowly turn to May
In drifting apple bloom I stand and ponder
  That spring should come and you be gone
    away.

Ben H. Smith, Illinois

To My Husband

How casually you take my slate and school
    books,
Meekly I follow you along the trail
That leads around the mountain to the
    schoolhouse
That gleams snow-white, out in the cedar
    vale.

You buzz a rock at a sailing yellow-hammer,
Toss me a rich persimmon on the way,
There is a pause; I hear your husky murmur,
'You are my girl, I'll marry you some day.'
Ah, love, how many times we've watched
    the glory

Of autumn burning bright upon the hill.
And though the years have turned my hair
    to silver
I am your girl, and love, and follow still.

Mary Elizabeth Mahnkey, Missouri

Deborah

A song of Deborah,
The wife of Jacob
And daughter of Eliphalet,
The sailor from Nantucket,
Blown inland and cast away on these untill-
    able hills.
Jacob, I remember as in a dream —
They took me by the hand and led me in to
    see him,
Bony, pale, and thin, lying on his bed,
Where he wrestled with an angel,
And the angel was Death.

And Deborah, who survived him,
I remember in spectacles
And gray hair tucked under an old ladies'
    cap,
Knitting vigorously.

And I remember a little boy
Who lived in those far-away years,
Running barefooted about the farm
And up the cow lane to the creek,

Driving the cows morning and evening,
Chasing the sandpipers,
Going to church in wonderful, copper-toed
            boots
And nodding to a fall on hot summer Sun-
            days
Between his father and mother in the high-
            backed pew.

Sometimes when company was coming,
And pies must be baked,
Deborah would take him elderberrying
Along the stone row by the cow lane,
And after the berries were stemmed and
            ready
She would read aloud from a small, leather-
            bound book of poems,
Then, closing her eyes and the book at the
            same time,
Would repeat from memory something
            about the Plowman and the Mouse,
Or Wee Willie Gray.

Oh, if one only had the copper-toed boots
To wear on Sundays, that would be some-
            thing!
Or find the little boy who ran barefooted
Up the creek after the sandpipers;
Or the leather-covered book
And a grandmother to read it,
And, reading, to lead one back as far as
            memory

Through the dew of a long-ago morning
To the dead that have never died.

W. W. Christman, New York

Spring Climbs High

Behold! the sage is bright and blossoming.
The cactus tips with red its silver spears.
The sun has cut creek banks with golden
        shears.
And wind and rain in sprightly chase
Dash swift across the mesa's grassy space.

Now wild pink rose, all color and perfume,
Blows sweet as Persian garden bloom.
Now meadow lark with clear, pure fluting
        cheers,
While on green hills white lambs are ca-
        pering,
To lilting notes re-echoing.
Lo! all the high country's apace
With spring!

Alta Booth Dunn, Wyoming

If We Could Hear With God

If we could hear all prayer with God
    At midnight when the hour is dim
And thanks go up for food and care,
    Ah, then, what joy to hear with Him!

But other prayers go up the stars
  From burdened hearts in every land.
In prison cells and golden rooms
  We see the upturned, begging hand.

He shares the sadness of our prayer.
  His palms are marked for each mistake.
If we could hear one night with God,
  Our hearts would break.

Brother X

Here I Shall Wait

You were longing for me again today: I
    knew
By the way the wind rippled the leaves;
By the way the mist formed in great drops
At the dawn and clung long to the eaves.

The wind was your hand in my hair; the
    rain
Was your tears that fell fast when we parted.
My own grief I kept 'neath my eyelids, but
    yours
Flowed freely enough, once it started.

After dawn I went out to pick berries. I
    found
Them in sweet and in wondrous profusion:
But no one set out with me upon the lone
    quest,
Nor lingered long at its conclusion.

The mimosa still blooms in the lane. I
    rested
A while on the bench at the turning.
No anger can dwell in a heart that is tender
And softened with hope and with yearning.

The mockingbird's young are full-fledged.
    She fed
Them with worms and with fruit from my
    bushes.
The old pecan tree is again glorified
By the nest of the merry brown thrushes.

I hung your old hammock today — it
    swings
In the shade of the oak trees. The shadow
Of the pine still models the head of the
    moose
As it falls, slanting-wise, on the meadow.

If you *must* dance, you must! But in time
You will come where your heart keeps its
    lover
And I shall forget these few sad lonely
    years
And kiss you a thousand times over.

It was here that I lost you, my dear. It is
    here
I shall wait for and find you ... if ever!
A love that binds two hearts together like
    ours
The applause of the world shall not sever,

You were longing for me again today: I
    knew
By the way the wind rippled the leaves;
By the way the mist formed in great drops
At the dawn, and clung long to the eaves.

Flossie Deane Craig, Georgia

They Pity Us

They pity us who turn the soil that it may
       breathe the sun and air again.
They pity us who see each new day born
       and see it die in glory.
They who, like us, were born to live a little
       span, choose four tight walls and
       concrete underfoot....

They pity us who walk on grass below, a ceil
       of blue above, and live like children,
       as God planned we should.
They pity *us!*

Mrs. Cecil D. Brown, Idaho

At the Funeral

She bends in awkward agony
    To kiss his cold white brow.
She hasn't kissed him in fifteen years —
    Hence the difficulty now.

Lorraine Mozee Taylor, California

Song

I'm glad my eyes may see the sun
    Of each fair day that floods the East,
That I may on the firm sands run,
    On simple, homely foods may feast;
That I have known the strain of care
    Reaped beauty from the things around.
Pressed forward with a will to dare,
    Have peace and sweet contentment
        found.
The storms have made my eyes more bright
    And pains have made the spirit strong;
The wrong has taught me how to fight,
    And love has taught my heart a song.

Rebecca Turner, North Carolina

Priest and Friend

*(Written on the Occasion of the 25th Anniver-
sary of the Rev. John I. Yellott as Rector of Em-
manuel Church, Bel Air, Maryland.)*

A priest of God, his table you have spread,

Have blessed the awful paten and the cup,

And we who dared on heavenly food to sup

Take at your hands the more than mortal
        bread;

Feeling around us our beloved dead

Who once were wont to kneel beside us
    there
Again returned the sacrament to share —
We rise up from the altar comforted.

We know and love you as our fellow-man,
Yet with a reverence no one should deny
The minister in that exalted place:
We're shaped by what we do; 'tis Nature's
    plan;
So Moses, coming down from Sinai,
Brought back a certain glory on his face.

A. F. Van Bibber, M.D., Maryland

In Memoriam

(*To My Father-in-Law*)

You would have loved this day, could you
    have seen
The willows dressing in their gayest green;
The way the winds from apple orchards
    blow
My tulips standing primly in a row.
You would have liked last evening's quiet
    rain:
The smell of freshness down the pasture
    lane;
And clouds of amethyst beside the gate,
Where faithful lilacs bloom a little late.
I have not glimpsed at Heaven but I pray
It is as beautiful as Earth in May,

As full of lovely things to see and touch —
So that you will not miss our spring too
    much.

Dorothy Wardell Boice, New York.

The Plowman

The frost bit deeper
Than the plow, and hard,
And driving through skin
Like a broken shard
Of steel that carried
An icy spell
Drew from the nostrils
The sense of smell.

But the man who bent,
Gripping the handles,
Saw the far sun lift
A thousand candles....
He saw the sun lean
To the springing grain,
Saw the suckling blades
In the kindly rain....

He saw men reaping,
And he saw men plod —
He saw in himself
A disciple of God!
Prophet and seer-wise
He saw the world drawn

In the pattern laid
Where the plow had gone!

James Chrasta, California

Another Year

*In writing this poem, I had in mind my father,
an aged farmer.... There is nothing else like it
in the world, that perennial resurgence of faith
and hope in the hearts of farming people....*

Another year the sun will shine at planting,
　　Another year the rain will come in June,
Another year the drought won't blight the
　　　　harvest,
　　Another year the frost won't come so
　　soon...

The other years are fleet and ever fleeter,
　　The ebbing tide is nearly out to sea,
And failing feet must once more tread the
　　　　cycle
　　To find what gifts from grudging gods
　　there be.

Dim eyes shall still behold the tall corn
　　　　growing
　　And phantom wheat shocks standing tier
　　on tier,
Red clover blooming gaily on the hilltop
　　In magic lands of hope, another year.

A. M. Walton, Illinois

II   *A MAP IN WORDS*

The Near Earth Rears Them

The near earth rears them: mothers with
    deep breasts
And quiet eyes that mirror naught but
    peace,
With heads unbowed by all the passing years
And love, unjudging, reaching out to help
Their children's talents or their faltering
    feet.

They are not city-wise. Their hands are
    rough;
The bodies clad in coarse and homespun
    garb.
Their days are long and hard. They are
    content
If they can serve the common needs of men.
They stand amid the crowd and yet apart,
Loving and loved, sturdy, serene, content.

The State that bred me is as one of these:
Her sons may perish but they dare not
    quail.

H. L. Whitcher, Maine

New Hampshire

A touch and taste of all that's naïve and
      good;
Enough of each, yet no gross amplitude,
A varied aspect everywhere you turn;
Familiar sights, yet ever new they burn...
Oh, who is there whose life has been well
      spent
Amid these granite mountain monuments,
Who will not say, as he who weds his bride,
I'll cleave to you, forsaking all beside!

Robert Fisher, 80 Years Old, New Hampshire

Prairie Hymn

O blessed peace that passeth understanding,
O mystic triumph of Gethsemane,
O holy hour when angel choirs are banding,
And evening's benediction falls on me!

I am at peace on prairies deep and rolling,
Where gentian blue and sunflowers are
      found.
When evening falls and weary feet are
      slowing,
How sweet is home! How hallowed is this
      ground!

Francis V. Stegeman, Kansas

Sonnet to This Soil *

O dark and ruddy soil! How could I
    know,
A child, that there was less of beauty there
Than shadowy trees, with moonlight-tan-
    gled hair,
And wild-plum petals, white as mountain
    snow —
The slanting, silver javelins of rain
No fear within my youthful heart instilled —
The mountain-laurel every law fulfilled —
And rhododendrons bore no guilty stain —

O rugged hills! Let strangers call you land
Of golden, stealthily-brewed contraband,
And hot and feudal bloods! But not that
    child
Whose bare feet pressed your meadows blue,
    your wild
Gray crags... and whose heart hunger yet
    has found
No sacrament, save your dark bloody
    ground!

Jessie Wilmore Murton, Kentucky

* *First published in The Louisville Courier-Journal.*

Storm and Kindness

I shall never cease to fear
Nebraska's blizzards,
nor to revel in the sweetness
of her springs.
And I shall forever rejoice
in the kindness
of her people.

Mrs. Blanche Pease, Nebraska

The Tired Land

In ill-won rest I lie stripped bare
Where vultures hang in yellow air.
Trains die away. All men move on.
Each creature fears my red-eyed dawn.
With choking dust I buy release
From human greed. I am at peace.

Eleanor Rhodes, Wisconsin

Montana

Land of the friendly handclasp,
Of doors that are open wide,
Of men who ride eagerly forward,
Ride 'em, Montana! Ride!

Sylvia M. Haight, Montana

Texas

This land I know is Texas, loved for these:
Glowing bluebonnets, gold of harvest grains,
The redolence of fragrant orange trees;
Booming oil fields; the mighty sweep of
      plains;
And for small children in whose radiant
      eyes
I see a greater Texas rise and rise.

Lavelle Maddox, Texas

III   *HERBERT EVERELL RITTENBURG*

Richer Things

I have forsaken myrtle bordered bowers,
　　Forgot the fragrance of the April breeze;
　　And I shall never grieve again for these
Nor vanished songs from unreturning hours.
Nor mourn dead leaves, flown birds, nor
　　　　withered flowers,
　　Youth's laden galleys gulfed in bitter
　　　　seas,
　　His bright wine swallowed to the last
　　　　dark lees,
His wasted lands and ruined, moldering
　　　　towers.

For all that I have seen is surely mine,
　　And all that I have been is mine today.
With every passing year a more divine
　　Resurgence of my spirit bids me say
That richer things than love or gems or
　　　　wine
Inhere in me and shall not pass away.

To My Son

These many years I've sought to shelter you
　　From what might seem to do you hurt or
　　　　wrong.
　　I've borne your burden when the way was
　　　　long,

Stood firm beside you when your friends
    were few,
Held shield before you while you struggled
    through
    The fight, and cheered your heart with
      martial song.
    In face of heavy odds and foemen strong
You've found me loyal chief and comrade
    true.

Ride on, then, lad, and hold our banner
    high!
    Though bitter be the brew your fate has
      poured,
Put all dark dreams and doubtful omens by,
Defy once more the unbelieving horde,
And sound our proud clan's ancient battle
    cry —
    Cast now the shield aside and use your
      sword!

Ready

With wild heart schooled to silence by years
    of toil and pain,
As my face has set to calmness against the
    wind and rain,
Unmoved by autumn splendors or beauty
    of forgotten springs,
I wait here on the hilltop the word the last
    hour brings.

A Letter

Thinking you will be interested, I am sending you news of the recent death of Herbert E. Rittenburg, two of whose poems appeared in your Forum. One of them, the sonnet beginning 'I have come back at last to my own land,' started your contest for the best poem in praise of one's home state.

His passing came suddenly, just when he was hopeful of success, so long delayed. The praise given his work in *The Country Home* gave him renewed courage and hope.

In his last letter to me, his friend, he sent me a rondeau that he had just composed, and also a quatrain, prophetic of the end. So passes a brave singer. — *Edda Ayers, Arizona.*

His last song, 'Ready,' is just above Mrs. Ayers' letter. We shall run others of his later if the pressure of living voices permits. We never knew Herbert Rittenburg except through the things he wrote: but we exchanged a number of letters with him personally, quite apart from the routine affairs of author and editor; and the news of his death weighs heavily upon our mind today. He was a very poor man, working as an itinerant hired hand; living, when ill health overtook him, with friends and relatives, doing the chores for his keep, and writing. There was some talk in our exchange of letters of his coming to Thorn Meadow and cutting briers in repayment for his food, bed, and tobacco, with time to write. But it was plain all along that he regarded this, and the CWA, and all such hopeful plans and projects as not for him. Ill, aging, a worn-out hand, he knew that his number was up. 'I used to be afraid that I should be a burden to others,' he wrote, 'but now I know that I shall not.' He was a man of invincible spirit and dignity. May he rest in peace....

[From THE FORUM — July, 1934]

From a Previous Letter

Hart, Virginia
August 13, 1933

... Many thanks for your kind words and for the invitation to 'come again.' I am sending you some shorter ones this time in the hope that you may find one you can use. I can always use the money! Still too hard up to manage typewriting. A man of my age (forty-eight) finds it hard to land a job in such times as these. Luckily, I am a person of simple tastes. So I manage to live.

I am including one rondeau in this consignment. I write many in this form and would especially like your opinion of this one. The others are chosen from what I think the best of my shorter lyrics. I have no key to what the reading public likes in the way of poetry. Very little of what I write seems to me to be the sort of thing that would appeal to the ordinary person of this generation. Young people seem to like my verse better than people of my own age do, although I consider myself something of a back number. Which encourages me somewhat.... I notice your letter was written in Washington, but I am sending this to New York as usual, and hope you can get a look at it by the next closing date... with many thanks for your interest....

As I Grow Old

As I grow old a sweeter note
Wells from each hidden wild bird's throat
And richer, brighter pigments dye
Each leaf and bud and butterfly,

Each sunset's many-colored coat:
I do not ask what these denote,
I know no proverb I may quote,
I make no comment, passing by
  As I grow old.

But this my lone, unguided boat
By greener islands seems to float.
The stars seem brighter; and more nigh
The dawn-glow in the eastern sky;
The harbor beacons less remote, —
  As I grow old.

Akin

The prairie, wide and desolate,
As fixed, as mobile, as the sea,
Is still the great sea's only mate,
The one partaker of her majesty;
And from their hearts the winds of fate
Draw forth one solemn song for me.

The bending grass, the flattened waves
That rolling dust and fog tread down
Still hide uncounted, unremembered graves
Of minstrel, warrior, slave and clown.
And dirges never heard in minster naves
Still wail to bitter skies their old renown
As, under watchful stars, the free
Wind holds grim revelry.

Unforgotten

I know not in what distant land
My dear one's dwelling place may be,
Upon what uncouth, alien strand,
Beyond what wide unfathomed sea,
Nor why we two must walk apart
Who fared together for so long,
Nor why the darkness in my heart
Should cast its shadow on my song.

I only know I love her still,
Shrined in my spirit's inmost deeps,
Some power greater than my will,
Through all the years, her image keeps.

The One Song

Is there no song that I may sing?
Waits there no perfect song for me,
After my lone, long wandering,

At the end of the last long trail,
Before the notes of my rude harp fail
In the silence of eternity?

Shall not one song be surely known
As mine, and yet have charm for others'
        ears?
To those who still must walk alone
And those who fare by busy ways
Through all their long, love-lightened days,
Bear grace of laughter and of tears?

Oh! be it simple, sweet and true
As that the morning gives the lark,
As old as life, and yet as new
As spring, or love! Lord, keep me strong
In soul, that I may hear my song,
And may it come before the dark!

IV   *W. W. CHRISTMAN*

The John Burroughs medal is given for the best piece of nature writing published each year. In 1934 it went to W. W. Christman. Few had heard of him up to that time. For sixty-nine years he had lived on a rocky hillside farm in Schenectady County, New York. On that soil he has made a living, raised nine children and sent them through school. He was over sixty years old when the last of the nine children reached maturity; then he started writing poetry.

He did not come to New York to receive his medal, but sent a message to the John Burroughs Association: 'I have lived on this farm all my life like an old tree. You could not transplant me now. Here the Arctic comes to me with shrike and fox sparrow, and the tropics with the returning birds in spring.'

Mr. Christman is a farmer in every sense of the word. As a boy he helped his father clear the rocky, wooded acres of the farm for cultivation. It was his father of whom he writes in the poem, 'The Untillable Hills.' The father's consuming passion was a hatred of weeds. The son rather likes weeds, and he loves trees. 'Before I die,' he told me, with a wave of the hand toward fields still clear, 'I hope to have the rest of these hills wooded.' As soon as he and his wife had no longer to provide for the children they began cutting down on farming operations. Only about twenty-five of their hundred acres are now under cultivation.

Down through the middle of his pastures runs a creek, the Bozenkill. Rising abruptly on one side of the Bozen-

kill is a wooded hillside. Here he has started a wild-life
sanctuary. Anyone is welcome there to camp or picnic.
He has around a hundred visitors some Sundays. The
Mohawk Valley Hiking Club has erected markers and a
lean-to, and helped him plant trees. On a bronze plaque
set in a boulder, the Hiking Club quotes a Christman
poem:

> I give, bequeath, devote, devise
> Shelter to every bird that flies;
> Harbor to all that walk or creep;
> To the red fox a bed for sleep;
> Table and roof for every guest
> And place for dove and thrush to nest.

Arthur C. Bartlett,
(Managing Editor of *The Country Home Magazine*, 1935)

POSTSCRIPT: Before he died further recognition came
to him, but it never disturbed him in his purposes and
ways. Robert Frost read some of his things, and came
to see him; this pleased Christman deeply. Later, in a
talk with the editor of this collection, Frost said: 'He's the
best poet in your book, and a man who does not face
Washington when he prays!' Christman kept on writing
to the end, publishing what he liked in *Trails*, a country
magazine put out at Esperance, N.Y. Two of his boys,
Henry and Lansing, are on the staff.

Most of his last poems were sonnets addressed to friends
who had gone on ahead of him, and the mood was never
wailing, but serene and sometimes humorous. He favored
the Shakespearian form. Consider the power and ease of
this final couplet:

> ... They have no sorrows, neither do they wake.
> Why should your heart be troubled for their sake?

Again, a jocund sonnet ended:

> ... Tonight if any ghost should walk the lane,
>   I'm wishing that it might be Sarah Jane.

Here is another, in memory of a hard-drinking old country doctor with a Quaker wife. Sober and repentant, the Doctor cries that if he had a rope he would hang himself:

> ... 'Thee'll find it on a nail out in the shed;
>   'Thee'd better double it,' his good wife said.

One evening last March (1937), Christman felt tired and left a poem unfinished on his work table. He went to bed and died in his sleep at the age of seventy-two. Surely the usual wail and fret of obituaries are superfluous here.

The first, and the last three poems in this section, and those from which snatches have just been quoted, are from *The Untillable Hills,** the book he left for his sons to gather together. 'Then softly fell the evening of content.'

R. L.

The Untillable Hills

> A small, silent, bearded man,
> With knotted fingers, hard and calloused
>   hands,
> And shoulders stooped with toil —
> But how he loved the earth!
> How patient he was with the untillable hills,
> Pulling and burning the stumps and roots,

* *The Untillable Hills*, 103 pages, with an Introduction by Robert P. Tristram Coffin. Printed by The Driftwind Press, North Montpelier, Vermont. Obtainable at $1.75 a copy from Mrs. W. W. Christman, Delanson, New York State.

Picking and laying the stone
In great walls around the fields
To protect his husbandry.
And most of his acres were hemlock soil,
        too —
Much poorer earth than he.

Sisyphus-like, for fifty years
He pushed a big mortgage uphill,
Meanwhile borrowing two hundred dollars
To send his brother out to Iowa
To be a professor in the agricultural college
        there.
And the two-hundred-dollar note he pushed
        for thirty-five years
Because the professor was absent-minded
And forgot to pay.
He had good reason to love earth rather
        than man,
And so God let him till it and love it
For more than four-score years.

He sat by the open window one morning
In his last spring, his hands folded,
(They were not hard and calloused any
        more,)
And his son was plowing in the garden
When the smell of the newly turned earth
        drifted in, —
'Oh,' he whispered to his nurse, 'if I could
        only plow again!'
He always wore cowhide boots

And would have felt uncomfortable among
  the angels.
I hope God had a few acres of rich bottom
  land
Not yet pre-empted when he arrived —
What a Heaven that would have been!

Career

Jeremiah Saddlemire
Lacked the Rule of Three;
The fact is that he never learned
All his A B C.
He said, 'The skool where gran'pap went
'Is good enuff fer me,'
And so when he reached fifty years
They made him school trustee.

The Schoolmate

Dear to my heart the unforgotten Junes
  When bubbling brooks of bobolink song
    ran high,
And in the upland fields the whistled tunes
  Of meadowlarks were poignant as a sigh;
And riper days are dear when she and I
  Came home from school on golden after-
    noons
While autumn lingered, and across the sky
The crows filed on to roost in long platoons.

And I have kept the country ways, while she
  Knew busy streets and heard the hum of
    life.
Once she came back and talked of time
    with me.
  They said she made a good man a good
    wife;
Her sons fought overseas; her husband died;
  A year ago they laid her by his side.

The Place Is Dear to Me

The place is dear to me whereon my father
Toiled in his prime and laid the hemlocks
    low —
It is such crops as these that I would gather
On land he cleared to mow.

Ira and Kate

In spring I've seen him with a sowing bag
Slung on his shoulder, sowing oats by hand,
His son behind him with the team and drag
Stirring the seed in that unfruitful land;
Often in winter with Kate sitting by,
We talked beside the fire while evening ran,
In summer helped him in his hay and rye
And never took the measure of the man.

And Kate — smiling and sitting in her chair,
With crippled fingers washing cup and
    plate,

Or with slow stitches at her mending
    there, —
Poor woman! smiling half her life at fate:
If sometime, somewhere, there is a reward,
Grant these two souls your greenest garden,
    Lord!

The Empty Cup

Time took her youth and scored her house
    of clay
And what is left lies here serene, supine;
The mourners weep — what more is there
    to say
Save that her house has not endured like
    mine.
Her thin gray hair — it was not always so,
Nor those shut lips no quips can move or
    part;
This was a splendid woman long ago
When she was young and April in her heart.

First love, the cup of wine, the sacrament,
The dear glad ways are over that were ours;
She is a shade and done with days and
    hours.
This is her clay and it is quite content;
It is a cup from which the wine is spilled,
An empty cup that cannot be refilled.

The Gift of Rest

Finale

The gift of rest be with you where you lie
Under the weeds and grass and the wild
  rose,
Or where steep acres run to reach the sky
And everlasting and heath aster blows.
Moss pink and blue-eyed myrtle thatch
  each shed,
Cover with beauty every house of peace
Where you who fell on sleep lie long abed,
Eternity the limit of your lease.

Peace be upon your houses! when you went
We grieved, we felt the bitterness, the lack,
Then softly fell the evening of content —
The world had changed, we would not wish
  you back.
Now peace be in your houses! soon we too
Must lay aside our work and rest with you.

V   *ALTA BOOTH DUNN*

Legacy

Though I am gone from here,
   Summer shall come again
   To bless with sun and silver rain
This garden place I've held so dear.

Within this green-walled space,
   Brown tang of loam shall rise
   On drowsy airs toward blue skies,
And peace walk with her olden grace.

And bush and flower and tree
   That I have made to grow,
   Tended and loved, each year shall glow
With bloom — for other eyes to see.

Song of Summer

Now Summer's tones are rich and soft
As earthy voices send aloft
A variegated glowing-tune.
Each mellow wind that passes
Among tall meadow grasses
Predicts their harvest will come soon.
Brown honey-bees zoom over
The musky white and crimson clover,
Praising the nectar with their croon.
Stalwart green corn in field
Is whispering of a Midas-yield;

Binder hums cheerily in tawny wheat
Of bread of life, so crusty-sweet.
A yellow apple strikes the ground
With low completed sound.
So Summer, to the country ear,
Pledges the bounty of the year.

Drought Harvest

I am the drought-tormented sod
And I call out to God,
'Why hast forgotten me
When Thou rememberest the sea?'
The gaunt hills echo back the cry —
Why... why?...

My bosom is lean and dry,
Withered by acrid winds' sere breath
And brazen sun's too-ardent touch.
O God, it is too long — too much!

I cannot nurture man or beast,
Or even of humble growth the least.
Unless Thou sendest speedy rain,
My sole increase is bitter bane,
My only harvest — mummied death.

(1935)

Rocky Mountains

Inscrutable
And unperturbed as God,
The mountains stand
In everduring majesty. No rod
Of Time is laid upon their backs. They
      band
Their noble heads with pure samite of snow,
But bravely naked go
Their rugged breasts to fanged winds
And brazen arrows of the sun.
By clear sweet wines
From glacial rills their parched sides are
      wet;
With beryl boughs of sempiternal pines
Their mighty thighs are fret.
Immutable
The Rockies stand
In shoes of ruddy granite, silver-set.
Look you, O my people! — but free
The head of gear and bend the knee
All reverently
In the presence of the high hills.
For are not the mountains His
Proxies?

After Drought

Now come the quiet days of cloud. Now
    healing hands of rain
Are laid upon the body of the stricken earth
    again.
The pastures bare and budding crops which
    met untimely death
When dragon drought belched forth its fiery
    devastating breath
On greening field and garden growth, on
    beast, and smiling plain,
And toiling man — all know relief from
    Summer's searing pain.

The farmer looks with new hope on his
    fields. With steady pair
Of grays he turns a furrow straight and
    black from gleaming share.
He stoops and breaks a clod. The soil is
    mellow, rich and deep —
'An earthy treasure here that Springtime
    crops will find and keep!'
He stands. And lo! — a promise bow
    illumes the misty East:
A sign that God has not forgot His man,
    His earth, His beast!

(1935)

Prairie Earth

Some day I shall return to prairie earth
    Where corn grows green and lush as
        tropic trees
    By golden shores of miracle wheat-seas
Surging from black stout soil that knows no
        dearth;
Where proud high poplars guard the
        staunch-built hearth
    Of folk who pledge their years to earth's
        increase,
And, faithful, reap a yield of plainsman's
        peace —
My father's folk, on land that gave me
        birth.

All my being remembers yet, and thrills
    To tall-grass sod. (O passionate and
        strong,
This Midland blood.) I'll leave these
        drought-seared hills
    For body's fare, soul's balm — before too
        long;
Before the final sleep I must go home
To claim my heritage of prairie loam.

As HER SONNET, 'Prairie Earth' reveals, Mrs. Dunn
is a midlander by birth. She went west and married.
Her writing is done between many other jobs. From

a mountain ranch, she and her husband have sent a son to college not to study Agriculture or Sanskrit or any one specialty, but to study, so far as possible, everything. As a writer contributing to the old *Breeders' Gazette* and other periodicals, Mrs. Dunn has made war for years on the notion that farming people and their young should attend to their business and let it go at that. 'I was down in Omaha with my son, Edwin, for a while last winter,' she writes, 'in the hope of getting a little sagebrush out of my hair and putting salt on the tail of some new ideas. After so long a time in the hills the sight of a streetcar well-nigh stampedes me, and even to ride in an auto has me pulling leather. Us old cowpunchers!' ... Whenever we have anything by Alta Booth Dunn in these columns, we feel that we are entertaining distinguished company....

(1936)

VI   *BEN H. SMITH*

Clouds of Gray

When we dug her narrow bed,
　　Buds were slowly waking.
Winter had her garment shed
　　For a last leave-taking.
And though April walks today,
　　Apple blossoms strewing,
Round my soul are clouds of gray
　　And a March wind blowing.

Then as Each April Smiles

Let me live close to the heart of things;
　　Sun on my face; wind on the clover;
Dew on the leaves where the wild bird sings;
　　Smell of the earth that my plow turns
　　　　over....

Give me a house far back in a lane,
　　A yard; and a child, singing with mirth;
Then as each April smiles through her rain,
　　There she will find me, close to the earth.

No Crown, Lord

No crown, Lord. No crown, Lord.
If in my life were deeds of worth
I only ask as my reward,
To keep the things I loved on earth.

I couldn't play a harp with strings
So long I've worked with spade and plow.
I couldn't find my way with wings;
I've found my feet, and trust them now.

But this, dear Lord, would please me best,
Better than harp or golden crown:
A little grass on the earth's warm breast,
And the chance to rest while the sun went
            down.

Unforgotten

Some things there are I can't forget:
    A field of wheat, a summer sky,
A rose the morning dew has wet,
    An old rail fence the road ran by,
A west wind singing in the corn,
    A smell of clover after rain,
The flushing east of early morn,
    The dusk of twilight in a lane,
An orchard rich in flower or fruit,
    The glint of sunlight on the trees —
Lay bare my soul and leave it mute.
    Lord, fill my life with things like these!

To My Mother

You loved the roses. I have heard you say:
'When the last door closes and I have gone
            away

'To that shadowed land from which there's
    no returning
'Let there be a rose beneath yon taper
    burning.'

And so tonight by the taper's gleaming
There is a rose in the twilight dreaming....
We go so soon.... Our words are but
    marks on paper....
I must close the door. A wind has stirred
    the taper.

At the Turn of the Year

The path we loved is quite deserted.
    Green nooks are bare
Where hollyhock with wild roses flirted
    In June's soft air.

An echo lives in this bitter weather
    Like measured song
Of two glad hearts that beat together
    When June was long.

Hushed is the eager rush and riot
    Of bird and bee,
And over all is a pensive quiet
    That cries to me.

So, like the dead rose now forsaken,
    I miss you much,
And love all things that can awaken
    Your voice... your touch...

Never a Grave Can Hold Me

There is never a grave can hold me,
  Be it ever so wide and deep,
For the dream of the living will tide me
  Over that silent sleep.

I shall dream of the redbud growing
  In a misty land of rain,
And I'll know by the wind's soft blowing
  When spring comes back again.

Music of the Earth

Tom was a fiddlin' farmer.
He knew land like a book.
Many a time I've heard him play
And it seemed to me he took
Part of the gold of sunset,
Part of the wind and rain,
All of the smell of clover bloom,
All of a field of grain,
All of the ripened harvest,
Part of all things that grow,
And put them all into a song
That quivered beneath his bow.

Fiddlin' or plowin' a furrow,
His heart was in his task;

Strength and the love of man and beast
Was all that Tom would ask.
Blunt was his speech, but ever kind,
Rough as the clothes he wore;
His fiddle cried of the things he dreamed
As we gathered at his door.
Tom was a fiddlin' farmer
That earned an honest praise
And back of his hoe and back of his bow
Were the dreams that filled his days.

VII   *RUDE RESPONSE*

O-h-h-h, He Fiddled

O-h-h-h, he fiddled with his hoe and he
    fiddled with his rake,
And he kept right on a-fiddlin' till his back
    began to ache.

O-h-h-h, he fiddled with his chickens and
    he fiddled with his swine,
And he kept right on a-fiddlin' till he didn't
    have a dime.

Wm. Helmar, Wisconsin

VIII   *BEN SMITH SINGS ON*

Campaign Song

(Played on Old Tom's Fiddle, to the tune set by Wm. Helmar)

O-h-h, Politics come with hue and cry,
They bring a plan and they praise it high.
They cry, 'Come here, Mr. Farmer Man,
We're back again and we've got a plan.
We're going to help you pay them notes
If you'll hustle around and bring in votes.'
So we work like the devil to help 'em win it,
Like Barnum's sucker that was born every
    minute.
When the thing is over and we have voted
It's the same old remedy sugar-coated,
And we find, instead of paying our notes,
They drive us home to feed the shoats.
But four years later they beat the pan,
And shout, 'Come here, Mr. Farmer Man,
We're back again and we've...' (*Repeat
    until tired.*)

Come, Let Us Walk

Come, let us walk this lane together,
Be happy 'ere this moment pass...
Ah, we are drunk with autumn weather,
Hearts trembling as the wind-blown grass...
Was ever there a sky seemed bluer?

Was ever such an autumn's gold?
Oh heart of mine, the earth is newer
Since you are mine to have and hold!

Defiant, Cold and Brave

I found a violet today,
  An early prophet of the spring.
It stood defiant, cold and brave
  In one small hollow's sheltering.

A light amid the winter's gloom,
  A song that murmured of the May,
A scent of orchard's drifting bloom,
  Was in that violet today.

Somehow it made me think of you
  Who are so brave through good and ill,
Who glimpse through clouds a rift of blue,
  And stand defiant, singing still.

Quiet Little Body

'A quiet little body,' they call you, dear...
They do not know the rivers flowing deep
That washed the sand-tracks over. In the
        old days we
Knelt at the rainbow's end and learned to
        weep.
Was it the poppy leaves that stained our
        fingers?

We held them to the sunlight and we
 smiled...
So long ago, and yet the memory lingers...
Love was so dear to us... and love was
 wild!

'A quiet little soul' I wrap that phrase
 around me.
I could be drowned forever in the sea
That flows from out your heart.... Since
 love has found me
I am but driftwood.... life may let me
 be....
'A quiet little soul' They don't know half,
Your little body hides... So, let us laugh!

There Shall Be Songs

There shall be songs when I have tired of
 singing of love and pain;
April will come with her soft rains bringing
 the flowers again.
Down these old lanes where you and I are
 walking beneath the bough
Youth will come again, and of love be talk-
 ing as we are now.

There shall be songs and their tone be
 clearer than mine can be;
Men will love again but get no nearer to
 life than we.

June will be here with her blossom glorious
    to crown each hill.
Somewhere I, over death victorious, will
    love you still.

Winter Songs of Love and Death

Why do I think of lilacs? It must be
Some part of you, a thought, a thing remote
That haunts me still and brings this scent to
    me,
Reminding me of lilacs at your throat...
Reminding me that Summer's richness dies.
And, O, how like the lilacs were your eyes!

II

Lo! in this world God places side by side
The little things Life brought for us to see;
Deep tears and laughter, hope that lived or
    died;
We as we are... we as we hope to be...
And when the winds of death strip bare the
    soul,
He takes the broken parts and makes a
    whole.

Notes

O, RARE BEN SMITH! His is an honest voice, and he
knows what he is singing about... What's the matter

with the radio people? Why don't they put him on the air? His voice would sweep this sickened land like a cleansing wind from the fields and sea. There have been plenty of patronizing 'folksy' farm programs edged with the exotic, rancid touch of Tin Pan Alley showmanship. The call now, as we get it from our mail, is for something real. Ben's mail address is Jonesboro, Illinois, if any big radio executive wants to know...

(1933)

.... ALONG WITH CHEERS, in general, we have a few complaints that Ben Smith has just about taken over the poet's place, above these columns, month by month. Other bards are muttering. From Minnesota:

O, Ben H. Smith of Illinois may sing to the Forum's *hoi polloi* songs of eternal love and mirth; but why give him the upper berth? Can Ben and his songs under no condition be exposed to competition?
                                                        A. Heinrich

Free competition, tooth and claw, thus far has been the only law we've counted on to choose and gauge the poems on this Forum page. We've cocked an ear to every air and run the grandest. *Laissez-faire* has been the watchword. Live and strive! Sing on; the fittest will survive. And now distraught poetic souls call out for centralized controls! ... Down, now, to prose: To keep things reasonably democratic we are going to limit him to two or at most three Forum opening songs yearly; but in order not to discourage Ben's initiative, the Editors have gladly bought a number of his poems, and will run them every now and then. Thus with a bow to the Right and a bow to the Left we press forward, or somewhere.

(1935)

...FOR SOME MONTHS NOW, Ben Smith has been pouring his poems, with prose interludes, down a local channel, a column called, 'Where the Hills Slope Upward,' in the nearby weekly *Jonesboro Gazette*. 'I'm as lost as a shoat in high oats,' he wrote us, when he first became a columnist; but later, 'I think I'm getting the swing of it better. I write it, and Al punctuates it,' he writes.

Albert S. Tibbetts, editor and proprietor of the *Gazette*, was born in 1858, the year that Lincoln and Douglas debated at Jonesboro. He was the oldest country newspaper man in Illinois. It was he who first encouraged Ben Smith to write, and set it, by hand, in the *Gazette*. He set Ben's first book, 'Lincoln at Jonesboro' in type and printed it, himself, by hand, in that one-man shop. He set Ben's column, by hand, admonishing him constantly to work some of his poetry over into his prose. The column has grown fast and struck down roots. Late this winter, Albert S. Tibbetts died. He was seventy-nine. Ben writes:

... 'I remember when Brisbane died I wrote a eulogy, and turned it in. His words had always meant something to me. Al read it and said, "I consider him the greatest apologist for entrenched wealth in contemporary history. But you seem to have seen him differently. We'll run this, as it is."

'Make what you can of the two poems about Al I am sending. They are the hardest two I have ever tried to write. He was so near to us here, so much a part of our life, that it seems something of me has gone with him.'

To an Editor

I

Here at his desk where the sunshine lingers
  Through the warm spring air,
White pages flutter to unseen fingers
  And we sense him there.
The old griefs rise as the vision passes,
  But the eyes still hold
The kindly smile behind the glasses...
  Our Al of old.

II

And this is life... that men must die to live.
  Each soul must brave the dark to find the
    dawn.
This is the greatest solace truth can give.
  Truth cannot solace me. My friend is
    gone.

(1937)

IX   *MORE BY BEN SMITH*

From a Letter

Jonesboro, Illinois.
Sunday evening,
September 16th, '34

There is always a little space of time here, between the close of summer and start of fall that falls like a benediction on tired nerves. I like it especially on Sunday afternoons, the peace and quietness of it, with time to rest and write. I will try to answer your questions the best I can.

I've been trying to write verse ever since I was knee-high-to-a-grasshopper. I have about as many more on hand as I have sent you. Any time that you care to look over them let me know and they'll be promptly coming your way. Yes, I have noticed myself that I often write the same poem under many different forms and titles . . . Much of my stuff has been written between work hours or at night when I should have been asleep. I did not get much schooling . . . came out of school when I was 13 years old and went to work . . . had to . . . My father went blind teaching school, and we had to pick up what he laid down . . . Been at it ever since and writing verse in the meantime . . . Been on this farm 18 years . . . When I get work out I make about $12 a week . . . This place I am on is a strawberry farm where the plants are grown and shipped to all parts of the country. I'm packing plants now when I work out which is about half time . . . I am 45 years old, married, with two boys, one 14 and one 19 years old. I would like to be able to buy a small place of my own even though it would be one or five or ten acres . . . I might go into the plant or flower business in a small way. A few acres and a three or four room cottage would be enough. With a place of my own, my own plants to tend, and time to write, life would be a long, glorious succession of Sunday afternoons!

I'm not much of a poet. I'm too near the dirt to fly among the clouds. I think that good poetry must be slow, drawn-out process. With me it must be written hurriedly or not written at all. I only know what I see and feel: and it is a poem if I have time to write it; if not, it gets away from me, and the harder I try, the more muddled up I get.

We had a full week's rain last week. Corn looks good and we're going to have enough of both kinds of potatoes to do us. And that's *something!* . . . I am sending you some more poems.

A Modern Sonnet

You smiled and I was interested,
But now, dear girl, you have me bested,
For pretty lips have learned to pout
And slender hands throw things about.
Love is no dream — I know it truly.
But say, what makes you so darn muley?
Why cry because with married blisses
Come fusses? What a muddle this is!

You say, 'O, well,' in half a dozen tones.
Skeletons grinning, rattle their bones,
Cupid's bow broken, he sits and moans.
Dead as the ghost of Davy Jones....

I wish that dam' radio 'd stop its clatter.
Hey, you cryin' kid, what's the matter?

This Was His Dream

This was his dream: That earth should
    give
More ripened fruit, of grain more ears;
That by his toil mankind might live
A little better through the years.

With patient heart he went his way
At weary tasks that knew no end;
Until at last there came a day
He died, and all men lost a friend.

But in his neighbor's orchard yields,
In roads and bridge that spanned the
    stream:
In richer harvests, well-kept fields
There lived a remnant of his dream.

To a Friend

'Life rushes us along so fast,'
O, friend, you say...
And yet it seems when it is past
We're just half-way —
So much that we have cried to see;
So much that we have tried to be...
God's love and peace abide with thee —
My prayer today.

Life rushes us along so fast
We scarce can heed —
The blossom-gracing spring just past:
The frost-scarred weed...
A day to live... A tear to lend:
A smile to give... A coin to spend —
God grant we meet again, my friend,
Where all roads lead.

At Candle Time

Last night at candle lighting time there
    came a low wind moaning
It sighed among the maple leaves as if a soul
    were groaning,
And down the lane we loved of old where
    dusky shadows lie
I saw your face for a moment's space out-
    lined against the sky.

Fred's Store

What's become of Fred Mayberry
Who ran the little store?
When all the folks in Berryville
Would gather at his door —

As one who held our heart and dreams
He went, and good deeds followed him.
He comes no more, and now it seems
As if the earth had swallowed him.

We've spent a many a pleasant hour
And talked on things galore,
While Fred weighed out the meat and flour
Our voices filled the store.

If Fred came back to Berryville
He wouldn't know it now;
The house is moved back on the hill,
A new store's there, 'and how!'

It sure has made things good to see;
But fancy oft recalls
The little store that used to be,
And Fred within its walls.

Autumn

Autumn like a tired man is sitting down to
       rest
Among the golden harvest by which our
       toil is blest;
The wind is singing in the corn that stands
       in ripened ranks.
To the Giver of the Harvest it is time we
       offered thanks.

Wind in the Hollow

Wind in the hollow,
You're singing tonight;
While ghost shadows follow
The trees robed in white.

He was so fair,
For him I would die.
And love is so rare
To such fools as I.

Wind, you are old,
As the sky overhead;
But you're never as cold
As love when it's dead.

Hope

Out of the wreckage of my dreams
I must build again,
Something to stand the winds of fate
And sorrow's rain...
One must have shelter though he cling
Blind-eyed to pain.

Farmer Dying

All things are still at last. The drone of bees
Is quite the loudest sound I've heard today.
I lie in peace. The ghosts of memories
Come to my mind, then softly slip away.

Not even reapers' song disturbs the air —
I heard them singing yesterday at noon.
Jim Brown's wheat's ripe... He told me it
       was fair.
It's over-ripe, unless he cuts it soon.

It seems so strange that I'd be lying here
While life goes on beyond my narrow doors;
But George is left... he's seventeen this
    year.
I hope he won't forget... to... do... the
    chores.

Wild Geese

Chill winds blowing,
Must you bring me sorrow?
Wild geese going,
You'll be warm tomorrow.
You will find the river
Where you fed of old;
I must sorrow ever,
For the grave is cold.

Once she loved to hear you
Calling from the mill.
Wanted to be near you.
Now she lies so still!
Tired out with praying
A long year through.
O, wild geese straying, —
Take my heart with you!

Cold winds blowing,
Will you bring rain
When buds are showing
And spring again

Brings her pink blossoms
To match blue skies,
And scatters the blue-bells
Where my love lies?

X   *BROTHER X*

Of All Good Medicines I Label Best

Of all good medicines, I label best:
These ringing winds; this windy sunset-
     splendor,
This elm tree curved in delicate surrender,
And moon-washed nights that touch the lids
     with rest.

Puddles like shields of gold designed by
     rain,
The snow on roofs, a single eagle feather;
Locked hands of friends who watch a fire
     together,
And men who fill the empty heart of pain.

To Losers of Earth and God

To all who lose the earthly touch
   I offer these:
A singing bird, a yellow fire,
   High trees.

To all who lose the sense of God
   I give the same,
But add to each one shining word:
   His Name!

Evidence

Some things have shone too gloriously
    near:
  Sun-yellow radiance after rain,
Lifting bent flower-tissue toward the sky
    again.
  I cannot fear.

I have too intimately known the thorn,
  The holy dark of bitter reverie,
Clinging to grass and many a wordless tree.
  I cannot scorn.

My soul has leaned mysteriously out,
  Touching the lyric flow of starry sod,
And smoky-silken hills beneath the heart of
    God.
  I cannot doubt.

Familiar Things

Familiar things have strength to brace the
    heart
When memory walks her dream-enchanted
    way —
Familiar roofs... grey barns... a clumsy
    cart...
Familiar snow on winter stacks of hay.

Now let us dream of old simplicities —
Of savory smells and candle-lighted walls,
Of cows to milk, of leafless maple trees,
Of lantern-gold and clover-scented stalls.

This fevered life will then be medicined
By drifting snow in flower-soft increase.
The chores are done and prayers are said.
    The wind
Now shuts us in and fills the world with
    peace.

Mountain Women

Here are these rimming mountains,
And this little red-roofed town,
With sunrise and sunset and moonlight,
And streets that go up and down.

Always and always and always
The old men talk and sleep,
But women too young for dying
Look out to the cliffs and weep.

They lean on brooms in the doorways;
The long freights pull and choke,
Writing of far horizons
In lines of golden smoke.

Little Towns at Dusk

The cottage lamps are gleaming
In little towns at dusk.
The lanes are soft with dreaming
And smells of honeymusk.

When tired boys are curled up,
Asleep as boys should be,
The chipmunks' tails are furled up
Inside a hollow tree.

A far-off dog is yipping.
The mellow shadows creep.
The little towns are slipping
Gently into sleep.

Winter Twilight

The autumn days are past
And winter days begin
To seal the river fast
And shut the lilies in.

The world is gold and white,
And frost enchants the pane.
The wind is out tonight
A-sowing silver grain.

The folk in heaven turn
Their star-lamps to and fro,
And cottage windows burn
Through flakes of falling snow.

Our Grief Will Pass

Our grief will pass when shadows throw
Their temple dusk along the snow.
Lamps will burn gold, and ever high
There will be calls and lullaby.

There will be tears, but long ago
Another wept and whispered low:
'This cup... Thy will be done!' and so
Whatever comes: To live, To die;
Our grief will pass.

The folk of earth have this to show:
From ice and dark, blue flowers grow;
From dull cocoons, the butterfly
Shakes out its wings to gild the sky!
In love and work and spirit-glow
Our grief will pass!

Note and Letters

THE SINGER is a country school teacher. A young
man, still in his twenties, he seems to have worked too
hard, and is now living West of his native Illinois; but as

soon as he gets his health back he will teach again. The following letter was sent to this desk with no thought of publication, but we have asked his leave to print parts of it:

Poetry has never been properly presented in the average classroom. Above all, I want to teach poetry and the poetic way of looking at life to country children. I majored in rural education at Columbia and Wisconsin. . . .

Everything about country education absorbs me — the seasons as reflected in schoolroom, boys and girls rosy-cheeked from long treks over the fields, corn-judging, milk-testing, socials, the very handicaps we have to rise above — old desks, inadequate stoves — these arouse sights and smells.

I'll never forget how I used to travel through blizzards on skis to my first school — sixty-seven youngsters in an old lumber camp town in northern Wisconsin. And my second school: it had worn out two teachers before Christmas. No books . . . crowded rooms . . . cold, flabby spirits . . . a real challenge!

But there were leaders among the dairymen in this unimproved district, intelligent, high-powered men who had never taken interest in the school because they had never been expected to. This story grows long; let me be brief by saying that we started a community club, and in one year they put in a new basement with a furnace-room, manual training and domestic science room, a lunch-room for civilized noon-day eating around a table. They decorated both classrooms and put folding doors between them, so that the entire school could be thrown into a large room for community meetings. . . . The Community Club did all this.

No city school could compare with that school for convenience and beauty. I can still see that white building with its long, gracious porch in front, set in generous grounds, with trees like a park, and a country church set directly across the road.

New problems have arisen in the rural field. New adjustments must be made. Now, if ever, the community clubs must keep alive ... everything that will help country people stick together in warmth of fellowship and help them over the hump of these difficult times. Our rural schools must be saved economically, and must be saved also from being standardized and becoming citified ...

(1935)

Further Correspondence

... I have had many good letters, straight and simply worded, from rural teachers and farmers about the poem and rural school letter that you printed. I want to sing straight from my most honest moods and impulses. I think that the little poetry magazines have made me too self-consciously literary. In their efforts to be original they often succeed in being merely pretty. My chief weakness is that I can't measure my own work. It seems to me that poetry is like personality; if you have it, nothing else matters; and if you haven't it's just too bad. But I can work and revise, and these letters from country readers have given me a lift ...

I have been doing some more work on the second stanza of, 'Who Die, Loving the Good Earth,' which was in the first sheaf I sent you. *That long tranquillity*, the sixth line of the second stanza, and the underlined word in the last line, made, I think, a strained ending. I thought of, *The dried leaf down the tree*, for the sixth line, and liked it for a while; but it seems to me now to confuse the figure; and I feel that the new sixth line and the new ending are better . . .

Who Die, Loving the Good Earth

For yet a little while
I hope my heart will thrill
To sunrise like the smile
Of God along a hill.
To bees in blue-eyed grass,
And dream-remembered places —
Delightful ghosts that pass
On children's upturned faces.

For just one moment more
I want my eye to span
From door to wider door
The legacy of man.
And when the last hour brings
A dusk on every tree,
I pray for stronger wings
To lift the earth with me.

——————— ——————— (1935)

From the Editor of This Book to Its Authors, in the Spring of 1937

I am happy to tell you that the Houghton Mifflin Company will publish a book of 150 poems by 53 country people; and I seek your express authorization to include the following of yours . . . . Mr. Van Doren wrote his Preface with no thought of gain, and my editorial work has been covered by a retainer. So (a most unusual feature in anthologies!) whatever the trade edition makes will be divided among the authors. Thus: There are 150 pieces in the book, and so 150 shares. If you have two poems in the book, you will have two shares in the royalties, etc . . . May I hear from you within thirty days, when I shall return from a trip West, and have proofs to correct? . . .

26 May 1937

Your letter to ——— ———, relative to some of his poems which you wish to include in what seems to be a new anthology has been sent me from ———, ———, for reply.

He whom you knew as ——— ———, entered a strict religious order of the Catholic Church more than a year ago, received a new name and has completely separated himself from the secular world and its interests. He can never of course cease to be a true poet nor cease the creation of poetry; but his work now is entirely spiritual and he has repeatedly asked me, his one confidant in the secular state, to tell any and all editors and publishers that he has no further interest in the magazines with which he was once concerned and above all prefers to keep his anonymity and be not bothered with correspondence.

His was not a happy life in the world. Now that he has found peace in the cloister and has given himself wholly to God, it would ill behoove us to pursue him to that hidden life and seek his poems. He has asked me to reply in this vein to anyone writing for information concerning him or for permission to use his poems. That being the case, I must ask you not to include any of his poems, nor his letter on rural schools, in your proposed book. This is not my request, but his, as though he had himself written you. I know he would ask me to add a thank-you for the wish of yours to include a number of his things in your book, and to regret that he must decline the privilege. Very cordially yours,

——————— ———————

28 May 1937

... Your suggestion that you run his poems anonymously
with brief note of explanation, would I am sure satisfy him and
at the same time not mar the collection. This is an excellent
way out of the impasse he has set up and your suggestion is
hereby accepted in his stead and for him.

I regret that I have caused you temporary embarrassment;
I was simply fulfilling the wishes of him who was ———
——— ... To preserve that requested veil I am pledged by
promise. I think I'd be giving his reaction were I to say,
regarding any material return on the book, that you simply
divide his share among the other contributors, or use your own
good judgement, should sales yield such return. Cordially,

——————— ———————

XI *YOUNGSTERS*

To a Tulip Bed, Sleeping

Far away the days and nights are coming to
     you,
  Spring is coming,
The pretty flowers are growing night and
     day,
  The horses are dancing;
We play and play.
  Warm days and nights are coming,
And spring!

> *Raymonde Plantz, Colorado. (She made up this
> song, at the age of five. Her mother wrote it
> down and sent it in.)*

June

June comes tripping over the meadows
  Clothed in flowers fair,
With slippers made of sunbeams
  And roses in her hair.

June comes bringing baskets of roses
  And strews them far and wide.
She drops them here and scatters them there
  Over the countryside.

> *Betty Alice Erhard, ten years old, Montana.*
> (1931.)

A Lament for Tall Ships

Tall ships! Tall ships!
  You've vanished from the sea,
And my heart keens a mourning song
  For your gallant company.

Tall ships! Tall ships!
  'Twas a needful life you led,
And the world could yet be using you
  And the race of men you bred.

Tall ships! Tall ships!
  Daubed with the sunset's flame
And glamoured with its romance,
  And nothing but a name!

Tall ships! Tall ships!
  That rode the oceans' surge,
The beating surf sings your funeral chant
  And green sea winds your dirge.

> *Robert L. Miller, nineteen years old, Ohio.*
> (1931.)

Sometimes, You Stars

Sometimes, you stars, I think you do us ill
  To beckon us to beauty, and to fill
Our little hearts so greatly. Man's but mud,
  Save for a touch of starshine in the
      blood.

> *H. J., twenty-two years old, New York*

We, the Inheritors

... These are the lands our sires
  Tore from the livid thorn,
Beating the stinging briers
  Back from the lifting corn.
These are the lands they held,
  Theirs from the siege with earth:
Are we the less impelled?
  Are we of lesser worth?
Not in the land we know!
  We are the land-born ones;
We are the ones to sow:
  We are our fathers' sons!

James Chrasta, twenty-three years old, California.

XII   *MARY ELIZABETH MAHNKEY*

Notes and Letters

It is with a special pleasure that we discover from time to time among the contributors to these Forums an old-time country correspondent. We were an old-time country correspondent once, ourself. That was years ago, but we formed at the time an admiration for country reporting which we still maintain. Nothing makes us so tired as to hear people, with a silly affectation of urbanity, deride their weekly newspaper and its reporters, and their intimate style.... Some of the best natural writing we have ever seen was in country weeklies, sent in free, or just about. The people who wrote it, did so because they were writers born; in them was stir of wonder and of curiosity which, however derided or unencouraged, must be expressed. A letter:

Dec. 9, 1932

I'm one of the faithful who scribble for our country paper, *The Forsyth Republican*. I have been at it ever since I was fourteen, and now I am fifty-four. I often add a bit of rhyme, nothing fancy. Like the other day, a fellow came down to our old mill and he had his old truck loaded with the neighborhood kids from out of the ridge, as well as corn to grind. So I said in my next week's items:

> When Andy Youngblood comes to the mill
> In that old truck of his'n
> The neighbor kids all pile in too,
> And then they go a-whizzin'
> Down to the old Oasis mill
> On Long Creek's sandy shore,
> Where they swim and hunt for pawpaws,
> And then they hunt some more.

I wish I was a little kid
Out on that pleasant hill,
To ride with Andy in his truck
When he goes to the mill.

April 8, 1933

... When I was a girl books were scarce, but I grew up with
the tattered remains of a grand old library that toured the Ozark
hills with us; for Father was always moving, though never very
far, from one farm to another, trading, and selling lands, you
know. So I revered a book and would walk miles to where
folks lived who had books, thinking they would loan me one.
But one unseeing soul gave me a cabbage to carry home with
me instead of a 'blame book' and I never did like her, nor her
folks. ...

Our study club here, working to establish a library, has
published 'Ozark Lyrics' in a booklet, locally, and they have
sold pretty well. ... We ought to have more local publishing,
done like that; and more respect for our little local newspapers.
The work I'm proudest of is what I've done as a country
correspondent; been at it forty years now, and always for the
Forsyth (Taney County) paper. ...

Lately, I have tried to concentrate on one form of verse,
something in keeping with surroundings. We have moved
from the old place into the county seat ... I went back there
the other day, and wrote:

They Couldn't Buy It All

It seemed as if the house were glad to see me,
    Still gently fragrant with the breath of her;
I felt a throbbing presence close about me
    As if of gentle, silver wings astir.

> And they were kind, these strangers now possessing
> This house that knew our love so rich and deep,
> As if they knew there was a hidden treasure
> They could not buy nor even hope to keep.

MRS. MAHNKEY has sung for us here before, but not for a long time now, and it is good to have her back... If you notice a rise in the farm mortgage figures, it is partly the fault of this department, for The Chair has bought a farm. The deed was delivered in a murky office on the Courthouse Square of Bel Air, Harford County, Maryland, on the last bright warm day before the onset of winter, 1933–'34: '21.96 acres of land, barns and dwelling, north of Churchville on the Priest Ford Road....' There is something strangely moving about a settlement of property; the seller yielding years of vital association, the buyer taking guardianship of strange earth.... Strange earth, but not, in this instance, alien; for Harford is next to Baltimore County, where we grew up. It is a land of low, slow-sweeping hills, rich in grass and great trees, abundantly watered, and rimmed with pleasant rivers which merge into the headwaters of Chesapeake Bay.... All through the droning legal rigmarole of the settlement a line from a poem contributed to these columns kept running through our head: 'I have come back at last to my own land.'... We bought the farm as a place to live and write. It will be a word farm. Our modest ambition is the biggest crop of words to the acre ever raised, even in Maryland. Our rotation will be words, words, words. Manuscript will be the one commercial crop. Those fields will rest in sod while we toil to add to the word surplus — a harmless one, we feel: one that does not bear hard upon the markets of those who farm for a living.... It may be a chance coincidence of experience, and no fair judgment; but we feel that Mrs. Mahnkey's poem, 'They Couldn't Buy It All,' is the best of the hundreds at hand, this month:

(December, 1933)

In May, 1935, we asked, 'Who is the best country correspondent in the United States?' and offered a $50 prize for the best clipping. Having read 1581 clippings, the first reader for the board of judges was nonplussed to find the local news of the lady who had in a sense suggested this tourney, incomparably the best; so he had the leading contending entries typed clean, with place-names and identifying marks obliterated or disguised, and the other four judges all picked the same — that of Mrs. Mary Elizabeth Mahnkey of Missouri. Response so exceeded expectations that the total awards have been increased fourfold, and the winner, if she wishes it, will be given a trip to Washington and New York... With a poet's instinct for the selection of significant detail, and with a beautiful simplicity of style, Mrs. Mahnkey not only tells the news but makes you feel what it means. Some of her items:

Oasis

The late rains that have advanced everything so wonderfully have not exactly pleased the tobacco growers as tobacco should be preparing itself for the knife, instead of trying to reach the sky.

Willie Snowden, a brother of Frank and Joe, came as an un-, expected visitor from California last week. He has been absent twenty-eight years. He said he could not resist the longing to see his mother once more, and the old home place. But the old house was gone, burned in a grass fire some years ago.

Steve Cline, who lives at Ridgedale, died Friday and was buried Saturday at Omaho, Arkansas. He was very old and in poor health, and had been a blind pensioner for some time. He had made his home with his son, Jesse, for the past few years. Another son, Chauncey, lives near here. Other relatives from Oklahoma arrived Sunday, too late for the burial.

(August, 1935)

XIII   *FROM OZARK LYRICS**
BY MARY ELIZABETH MAHNKEY

* Published by the Taney Hill Study Club,
Forsyth, Mo., 50 cents.

After-Glow

Playthings again on my kitchen floor,
A brave cookey man to make once more.
And the old coffee mill is a wonderful thing;
He hauls it around on a gingham string.
And, resting my cheek on his curls of gold,
I forget I am gray, and heavy and old.
And forget that 'tis 'Granny' the sweet lips
      say
Instead of the 'Mommy' of yesterday.

My Poems

They come when I am churning
Or when I'm making bread,
Or when I'm hanging out the clothes,
A-dancing 'round my head.

Like flocks of yellow butterflies
A-dancing in the sun,
And with clumsy, toil-worn fingers
I try to capture one.

But I mar the gold-dust beauty
Of the fragile flut'ring wings.
I cannot capture butterflies
But I love the joyous things.

Ridge Runner

If I could live on White Oak Ridge
   It seems to me I'd ruther.
These river fields so rich and green
    They cling, an' clutch, an' smother.

I love to feel a clean high wind
   That whips the leaves together,
An' watch the lights in far-off homes
    Dance through the rainy weather.

What little breeze comes in this way
   Is hot from heavy tillage.
How cool the shady dooryards
    In my little old home village.

This stiflin' corn shets off my breath;
   I'm tired of rakin', mowin'.
I'd ruther ramble down the ridge,
    See huckleberries growin'.

Two Dresses

I had three dresses,
Now I've got two
Fer the plain little white one
Trimmed in bright blue
I cut into garments

So tiny and small
Fer my pore little baby
A-comin' this fall.
The boy that I wush'iped
Tole me black lies
An' run off an' left me
With tears in my eyes.
O pore little baby
With no name at all.
Mebbe God'll fergive me
An' hep us this fall.

When They Killed Jim Lee

I loved the tales my grandsire told,
When life was wild and free
And in the Ozark Mountains
He rode with Jimmy Lee.
Dearer than a brother
This youngster seemed to be,
And I can't forget the story
And the way he looked at me.
His stern dark eyes so wild and fierce,
His hand clenched on his knee —
'Now listen, boy, 'tis a sorry tale
Of how they killed Jim Lee.

''Twuz at a dance at Hampton's.
We wuz havin' a peck uv fun
When a gang come in from the river
An' thought they would make us run.

Some fool shot out the lanterns —
We fit thar in the dark,
Gals an' wimmen a-screamin'
But none of us missed our mark.
Then, some one ripped the paper
Off'en the cabin wall
An' lit a blaze in the ole fireplace
Jest as I seed Jim fall.
A tall slim cuss bent over him,
I seed a long knife shine,
But I wuz as quick as the stranger
An' he tuck the blade uv mine.

'Jimmy died jest about mornin'
Holdin' my hand 'til the end,
An' he grinned when they come to tell us
That down the river bend
They wuz makin' a long, long coffin
Fer one uv the river men.'

XIV   *MORE BY MRS. MAHNKEY*

In New York

What shall I do in the city,
   I with my mountain tread,
With arms that are bramble-torn
   And hands that are coarse and red?

Lost without my apron
   And familiar old milk pail,
Bewildered, frightened, homesick,
   Far from a mountain trail.

Give me thy strength, O City,
   That I may walk at ease
Among the throng of strangers
   As I do 'mid friendly trees.

Give me thy secret, O City,
   To carry home with me
That I may bring my neighbors
   A taste of this ecstasy.

Question

Could I have been in Maryland
Down by the Chesapeake Bay
And did I see that cloudy mist
That softly, lightly lay
Along the gently rolling land
That holds the restless sea

Where wide-winged birds still utter
Their plaintive threnody?
I know I was in Maryland
For deep within my heart
There is an aching sadness
That comes when friends must part.

Back in the Mountains

I'll take down the old clock.
It's been there forty years.
I'll wrop up pappy's picture
While I wipe away the tears.
I'll pack the old blue dishes
That wuz brung acrost the sea.
But O, my grand old walnut
I can not take with me.
Here Sissy had her play house
And Johnny had his swing,
And here the mocking bird first come
To tell us it wuz spring.

Cherry Pies

This is her kitchen, where she worked and
    sang
And from the little window looked away
Down to the river, veiled in gauzy mist
Along the little fields of corn and hay.
Here she was busy, making cherry pies

When stricken with the shock of child-birth
      pain.
With white set lips, she finished here her
      task,
Then dragged her weary limbs to bed again.

Cherry pies, in scented rosy rows,
The women stood and gazed, with dripping
      eyes.
'She was so peart, an' now that she's been
      took
Jay Jones will miss her, and her cherry pies.'

This is her kitchen, where she looked away
To what bright glory on that summer day?

Destitute

'He was so good,' she sobbed
Beside his casket there,
While their little children crowded near
To whisper and to stare.

I saw his banjo on the wall,
His red hound in the door,
His rifle in the deer-horn rack —
Just these, and nothing more.

But as she kissed his cold rough hand
I knew and understood
The simple love that made her rich,
'He was so good, so good!'

Do Not Forget, My Dear

Do not forget, my dear, that he is mine,
Although you clutch and cling and hold and
      twine,
He will feel hunger for my salty batter
      bread,
Feel yearning for his cool, hard attic bed.
He loves the fight with wind and snow and
      rain.
He never knew satiety's dull pain.
I know what made that scar on his round
      chin.
I know that hollowed arm that you lie in.

Do not forget, my dear, for I shall come
Into that heated, scented nest you've made
      his home
And take him with me, while you moan and
      weep,
Back to that attic bed, where he can rest and
      sleep.

Hollyhock Tea

When I grow old, I'll raise turnips
And try to like turnip stew,
But now that I'm young, I raise holly-
      hocks
And asters, and marigolds too.

Raising turnips is stupid,
That is why I dread growing old,
Do you think I could live on hollyhock tea
Or shop with the marigold gold?

Perhaps my flowers will remember
And make intercession for me,
That old age will come along gayly
And help me make hollyhock tea.

XV   *OTHERS LIFT THEIR VOICES*

Prayer of the Homesteader

Oh, gently, thou Nevada,
   Take these seeds I give to thee
And care for them most kindly,
   So they may grow to be
The common garden flowers
   That shall mean home to me.

I do not ask a treasure
   From thy gold and silver loot,
But only that you nourish
   This tender, living root,
So it may sometime grow to bear
   The tempting, luscious fruit.

And now, O grim Nevada,
   I'll plant my seeds and pray
That you may learn to love them
   And cherish them each day,
So that this bit of desert land
   May be my home alway.

Pauline Lattin, Nevada

In Clover

This hot day I lie in the grass
And smell the clover and see the bees pass

From blossom to blossom methodically,
Taking no notice at all of me;

I shall garner their honey when summer is
    done
And taste what they worked for under the
    sun,

And just for a moment I'll smell the clover
And close my eyes, seeing the bees pass
    over.

Elisabeth G. Palmer, New York

Last Night

When in the dark last night, against the
    windows
    I heard the silver rhythm of the rain,
There woke in me old ecstasies and longing,
    Forgotten dreams stirred wistfully again.

I thought the heavy years had stilled their
    calling:
    I heard them in the muted rain last
    night —
Sweet as remembered scent of yellow roses,
Dreams that would turn to ashes in the light.

Mildred Ann Hobbs, Kansas

Winter Settles Down

The fields and hills are white tonight, I
    know,
    And all the lanes and roadways drifted
    deep;

The bitter north wind croons across the
  snow
  An eerie chant, to still the earth to sleep.
And trees wear shining armor of the sleet,
  But I remember purple fields of June,
A sudden burst of lark-song, piercing sweet,
  A bough of leaves across a yellow moon —
When brooks lie bound in glittering chains
  of ice,
If I can still remember summer's glory,
  And know that June will surely come again.
Then I shall trust the tales of Paradise,
The peaceful land of sweet old song and
  story,
  Where there is no more death, no grief nor
  pain.

Mildred Ann Hobbs, Kansas

I Am the Plow

I am the plow.
My steel nose rips the earth in dark and
  loamy ribbons.
I hum a clean song.
I spread a new blanket to protect earth's
  sleeping granary.
I open new treasure — an ageless garden
  ever new
That keeps man's belly full.
I am the plow.

A. Heinrich, Minnesota

Open House

My door stands wide in the sun and rain
  And my friends they come from far,
One is from town, and one from the West
  And one from where tall ships are.

H. L. Whitcher, Maine

Here in the Marshes

Here are cowslips wading
  In the marsh, waist-deep
And silver willows standing
  Where the marsh waters creep;

Oh, the woods are lovely
  When the green buds burst,
But here in the marshes
  The spring stops first.

Elisabeth G. Palmer, New York

Autobiography
[The Collected Rimes of a Writer Born in 1895,
Condensed, and Dated]

I. First Song. 1915

Bugles, angrily blown and shrill,
  Challenging pride,

Even to death, with honor still
  Unsatisfied...
Moonrise, mist on the meadowlands,
  Ships on the sea,
Tempest, and beautiful folded hands
  Tell me of thee...

II. Private. 1917

The day we marched to take the train
The crowd was dismal as the rain.

Their very silence seemed to cry,
You all will die. You all will die.

Our singing step (one-two, one-two),
Laughed all the way, *And so will you!*

III. Song of Training. 1918

They wake us sometimes from our soundest
    sleep,
Old dreams, by day forgotten; overlain
With time and training. They awaken us,
And make us wonder that we are afraid:

That we should fail to hearten to a trade
That joys in strength and singing takes its
    chance
Where youth triumphant against kings
    arrayed

Sunder the ancient bonds of circumstance!
That knows quick life, that leaves a shining
          blade . . .
We wonder if we really are afraid.

And soon we find ourselves so calmly bent
Upon dread certainties, and imminent;
So mindful, too, of all that need be paid,
We wonder why it is we're not afraid!

IV. Sergeant. 1918

Some roads they count it not a sin
To lead a soldier to an inn
Where man may rest and ease the heart
With laughter and red wine.
Such was the road to Poitiers,
And we were rich, and we could pay,
And own the place and kiss the maid
At every swinging sign . . .

V. To Heroes Who Write War Books. 1919

When war has all the world ablaze
    And boys go grinning forth to die,
That is the time for battle lays,
    That is the time to sing the lie!

But now that all the fires have died
    And only bitter doubts remain,
Stand forth to show the world you lied
    And make us face the facts again.

VI. Class Poet. 1920

Behold! how swift the matter is effected,
Bards spring full-blown to being in a day.
In truth, 'twould be Democracy perfected,
If only we could turn them out that way!
But 'tis not true. Forever and for aye,
Poets are born, alas,— and not elected....

Enough! We chime the dole of men to dwell
No longer by these blue Cayugan streams,
And trumpet stanzas vauntingly to tell
A busy world of stratagems and schemes
New men are coming, new in flesh and
        dreams,
To bridge the deep, and rear the citadel....

O, pleasant land of many an olden tale!
Aye, more than that; more than our hearts
        can tell,
Your shore lies in the sunset, and our sail
Tugs in the winds that to the morrows
        swell.
Friend parts from friend, and all from thee,
        Cornell,
Go forth to life! Cornell, farewell, and hail!

VII. Desk Job. Springfield, Mass. 1921

All you who love your work to do
    The best of anything,
Take heed, I pray, to shelter you
    From suns and winds of spring

Which pour such wine as tempts a man
  To sloth and waywardness
And lead him mockingly to scan
  Position and Success.

Those struck by sun in springtime may
  Forever bear the blight.
'Tis safer far indoors to stay
  On days like this, and write.

VIII. For L. v. L. 1922

... And now by all the stars returned to
    visit
  Valleys remote and dreaming, high and
    fair,
Appears a gracious lady and exquisite,
  Walking in white with jewels in her hair.

IX. An Hour's Work. (Read to a 4-H Club Conclave by a Fledgling Extension Professor at the Ohio State University.)
1923

They'll ast me, 'What you been so long
    about?'
And, 'Don't you know that supper's on the
    table?'
And, 'Do you think you ever *will* be able
To get the water to the pigs without
Being an hour about it?'... What if I
Would answer out my mind? What if I'd
    say:

I fed your pigs and then took ship away
To visit all the islands of the sky
That sunset makes. A hungry polar bear
Swum after me but I got safe ashore,
Climbed mountains, built a palace, fought a war,
Got married to the leading princess there,
All in an hour... Don't it seem to you
I did right well to get the pigs fed, too?

X. *The Professor is Homesick. 1923*

When I am old and all my days are ending,
    I shall return to things a part of me.
To little hills and valleys soft descending
    In merging undulations to the sea;

Mists from the sea, blue mists, at twilight
        creeping,
    To sleep upon the valley's rounded arms;
Stars close above the hills forever keeping
    A near, familiar vigil on the farms;

Wide farms and rich, their gleaming acres
        swelling
    On hill and vale to plenteous increase;
Homes deep in oaks; a quiet people dwell-
        ing
    In kindliness and reverence and peace;

Old roads in peace with shining rivers
        wending;

The meadow-path and locust-scented
    lane;
Roads to the sky with slender trees attend-
    ing —
    I know that I shall tread these ways
    again.

XI. Extensionese. 1924

Omitting all detail, we may say in summary that this Extension organization made
face-to-face contacts with 1,347,249 persons in the past year. *From an Official Report.*

Behold! A sonnet is a Piece of Work
    Projected, Planned, Directed, Supervised
    From Concept to Objective; Organized
In Scope and Form and Function...
    (Never shirk,
O Muse, the Follow-up! Aid me to seize
    Each Step and Aim and Goal! Co-
    operate,
    Commune, Confer, Concur, Coordinate!
A little Splendid Spirit, if you please!)

Answers my Muse with ribald snickers: 'I
    Have just been reading the report above.
    Sweet cats and dogs! Ah, me! Great land
    o' love!
It makes me snort and giggle, sniff and
    sigh,
How Educators can take words and twist
    'em....
Face-to-face contacts! God! They must
    'ave kissed 'em!'

XII. *Engaged to Kate. 1924*

O! Arrogant April and indolent May
  Have kissed and cavorted and scampered
    away
  To be with the happily married who stay
In the lands beyond the moon;

And born of the union are winds in the
    trees
  That whisper of parting and murmurous
    seas,
  And heart-shaking beauty — and verses
    like these
To June!

XIII. *Christmas and New Year's Card, 1924-'25*

The elevator man calls out the floors
In gladsome tones and winning, and the
    grim,
Erstwhile relentless janitor implores
That if we don't get heat to just tell *him*.
Salvation Army pots go jing-a-ling.
The man in '7' offers me cigars...
Afar away the quiet church-bells ring
And dreaming cedars reach to touch the stars.

By city signs and omens, then, we know
'Tis Christmastide; and high above the
    din

Of towered Gotham send a wish or so:
Snow to your roof tonight, and peace within;
And all the joys the season can afford.

Mr. and Mrs. Russell Robbins Lord

XIV. End Paper of 'Men of Earth,' a Book Finished in
      New York City in the Winter of 1930

Here are old graves of men and women
      forgotten.
Their hills have taken them back; their
      blood and bones
Have gone in the rains the way all flesh be-
      gotten....
Let us trace their names on the stones.

They farmed. Their harvest is over. Now
      they slumber;
Their women beside them quiet; all passion
      spent.
The days of their seedtime and harvest
      have run their number,
The days of their discontent.

Sleep, then, George, James, Ann and
      Priscilla Nevin,
Do you know that your dust is the food of a
      silver tree,
Lifting white arms in April, flaunting to
      heaven
Triumphant banners of eternity?

R. L., Maryland

Party Line

Hello, Central! Four-o-four.
Say they won't answer? Ring once
    more....
Hello, hello! This Cinda Mae?
Well, how are you today?
We-ll, that's too bad.
Ain't this weather enough to drive you
    mad?
Are your hens a-layin' any?...
Well, anyhow, they ain't worth a penny....
Just listen to those receivers comin' down.
Every word we say'll be all over town.
Well, I never say to their back what I won't
    say to their face,
And I don't approve of the way the Joneses
    are raisin' their Grace,
Runnin' to the pitcher show most every
    week;
But you know they all got a wild streak....
And them Brown boys'll land in prison yet,
Why, I've seen 'em with my own eyes
    smoking a cigaret....
Well, sorry you ain't feelin' well;
Hope you don't get down abed;
And Cinda, remember, not a word of what
    I've said...

Jean Stansbury, Illinois

Hail to Mud!

Come bend the knee to the fertile Mud,
Divinest ruler of royal blood!
Wheat and barley, oats and beans,
And a host of growing greens,
Gift of his consort, Spring, our Queen,
  Hail to the Royal Mud!

Sow the grain and hoe the spuds,
Tho' propaganda o'er us floods.
Let brain trusters do their derndest,
How to eat has long concerned us,
  Crown the Good King Mud!

Hear the thunder's threatening thud.
There'll be miles of mushy mud.
F.E.R.A., Alphabet soups —
Feed them all to the Boop-a-doops,
Hip, hooray, and one more whoop!
  Hail the Good King Mud!

Frances V. Stegeman, Kansas

I Have a Little Son

I have a little son who talks of war —
Feet spread apart and sparkling eyes: alert,
He hears the bugle call, the rolling drums
And joins (to him!) the joyous marching
      feet.

Again he sits astride a splendid horse
And charges 'gainst the fierce onrushing foe.

My heart leaps in my breast and skips a
          beat.
I turn to hide the stark fear in my eyes.
Then, quietly, I face him with a smile
And tell him with what words I may com-
          mand
That *now* we're planning peace. No longer
          shall
The rich and fruitful nations be at war,
But all must work, and for the good of all.

Blank disappointment fills his shining eyes
That stare a wistful longing back at me:
'But listen, mother, if they *should* have wars
When I am big, they'll surely call for me?
Won't they need me to help them win?' he
          pleads....

An agony of terror grips my heart:
Those beaming eyes! those tender baby lips!
Did I give birth to this sweet flesh
And must I bring it to a rich maturity
To feed the glutton War?
Dear God, he does not see the pooling blood
Nor hear the cries on sun-baked battle
          fields;
Nor does he smell the rising stench from horse
And man left there, a feast for filthy birds —
All rotting carrion — and must I show him
          these?

Days pass and naught I hear of battles
Till a show: or, perhaps he reads in history
Bare facts laid down, and instantly
His fertile brain supplies details of color
And the action there! A quick compelling
    march
Upon the air, a bugle call — and up his arm
    will go
And high his voice is raised to cheer his
    hosts
To follow him to glorious victory!
'Gee, mother, won't I have to help them
    win?'
I have a little son who talks of war.

Flossie Deane Craig, Georgia

Thanksgiving Hymn

Happy am I when the year brims over
    And a ripened harvest hides earth's
        breast,
Whispering corn and billowing clover
    Sing to me through the night's long
        rest.

Edda Ayers, Arizona

Farmer

I am at peace. What is life's goal
But peace of mind and heart and soul?
How good to lead a peaceful life,

With heart kept free from hate and strife!
I've worked with heart and head and hand,
Paid all my debts and tilled my land,
I've earned my bread by sweat of brow,
Driven the team and held the plow.
Little have I of worldly wealth
But rich I am with home and health.
God meant that men should work and pray,
I am at peace. At peace, I'll stay.

Enoch C. Dow, Maine

Porch Song

I am at peace, the chores all done.
The smell of drying hay floats on the air.
And you are here, beside me, on the porch,
While tinkling bells of cattle lull my care.

I am at peace. The crop is good this year.
We'll pay the note down at the bank
And buy a separator for the cream.
Our kids will go to school this fall
With brand new shoes.
And you shall have a dress that's soft,
My dear——

I am at peace,
The chores all done
And you are here, beside me, on the porch.

Agnes Foster Salmon, Washington

Wagon Train Minstrel

I meant to stay and finish the plowing and
    planting,
But the wagons crept past on the road
    leading over the hill —
The long brown road, and my fiddle beside
    me chanting,
And the voices that whispered within me
    and wouldn't be still:

'You can bow a brave song for throats too
    dry for singing,
Jig for the sick child on her trundle bed,
Conjure from strings the sound of church
    bells ringing,
Fiddle a requiem for the tired dead.

'Lift lush green meadows and the swift
    brook's laughter
Before grim faces lifted to the height,
Catch up your dreams, jongleur, and
    follow after!' ...
I am at peace making songs by their fire
    tonight.

Alice Shefler Martin, Washington

Freedom Is Lonely

Freedom is such a lonely thing!
A bird high on wing —
An unknown waterfall deep in a wood —
To whom are these things good?

Loosing our bonds and throwing off a load,
Walking an unknown road
Not pausing or down-looking for the small,
Our own selves all . . .
Oh, it is better to be loved in spring!
Freedom's a lonely thing.

Gertrude Scott Jewell, Ohio

Cradle of Peace

The Eve of Christmas: to the still, dark barn
With lantern dimmed against the wind, I go
To see if all is well. The lantern weaves
Strange mystic wheels of yellow light that
      glow
On cows asleep; their udders pink and
      puffed
With milk, lie pressed beneath them.
      Everywhere
The pungent smell of hay and warm cow-
      flesh . . .
White hens deck stanchions like plumes
      fastened there

And drooping from some pageant long
    delayed.
Paws folded on their breasts, two kittens,
    lost
In sleep, lie by the wall. Through that
    cleared space
On yonder window, hung with lace of
    frost,
Too fine for God's, Queen Venus drops her
    wand
Across a manger sweet with clover hay....

A rich content is here and over all
A gracious royal presence seems to sway,
And misty halos of sweet earthiness...
A calf bleats in his sleep; all noises cease...

Not such a mean and squalid place, a barn,
To be the cradle of a King of Peace.

Marion S. O'Neil, Montana

Call Home the Heart

Call home the heart from wandering, and
    know
   Through all the years
There is no thing but this: laughter and
    love,
   An hour for tears.
Birdsongs at dawn, sunlight and firelight;
   Small feet that start

Uncertain journeys. There is nothing
    more;
Call home the heart!

Frances Davis Adams, Arizona

The Tamed Drake

The farmer's son had found
  The drake with a shattered wing
Where it had hidden in reeds
  To die by the pasture spring,
After the flight had gone
  And the hunter had sought in vain.
The boy had lifted the drake
  And tried to soothe its pain.

The wild heart beating so fast
  In his hand made him afraid
That it would break, and the eyes
  Were jewels of pain as he made
His way to the barn. With splints
  He bound the broken bone
And found an empty stall
  Where the drake would be safe alone.

He brought it water and corn
  And left them close on the hay,
And hoped it would drink and eat.
  His father called him away
At dusk. For many days
  He tended the drake, and the wing

Was healed and the drake grew tame
   And ate what the boy would bring.

The wings that had dipped the glint
   From lakes of the northern star
Were clipped, and the drake was free
   In the yards and he wandered far
From the white ducks of the farm
   And would flap his wings and cry
And turn his head to the side
   And look long into the sky.

A shadowy line through the mist
   Of early spring and a call!
And out in the yards the lift
   Of the drake's wings, fearing a fall
At first! Then the strain and the flow
   Of the wind and a dart on the skies!
And a boy — who had let the wings
     grow —
Standing with tears in his eyes!

          Glenn Ward Dresbach, Illinois

Corn Song

Across the April valleys run
Long black furrows, one by one;
One by one till the broad fields lie
Plowed and rich to the April sky.

Within the sound of a river singing,
   The corn blades dance, for a sweet year's
     bringing

Food, to the hungry sons of men —
Life, that there may be sons again.

By early August the tall corn hides
The height of a horse and a man who rides,
Rides by the singing river's sod
And sees in his work the work of God.

The whir of a quail, and a ground mouse
       burrows
Under the corn in the long dry furrows;
There is frost in the air as the golden grain
Finds its way to the crib again!

Benjamin Wallace Douglass, Indiana

Singing, the While You Work

'My faith looks up to Thee,' your clear
       voice rang,
As you set shining milk pans in the sun.
I like to think of that old song you sang,
Not knowing that earth's work was nearly
       done.
The farm beasts seem to know that you are
       gone,
Your collie grieves beside the open door.
The black cow lows across the bars at dawn
And time runs past much as it did before.
Within the neat farm kitchen other hands
Are busy with the little things you left
When your bright spirit ventured to far
       lands,

Leaving my world of happiness bereft.
And if the God you served so gladly here
Sets homely tasks for you that some might
          shirk,
I know that at some bright morn I shall
          find you, dear,
Singing, the while you work.

Gladys Ray Snakenberg, Ohio

Home From Town

The road from town was sweet with clover
          blossoms;
  I'd left behind the city's grime and heat,
But not the thought of hungry little faces
  Of children playing on a noisy street.

My rosy youngsters met me at the gateway
  With buttercups they'd found beside the
          stream,
And there were golden muffins for our
          supper;
  A bowl of strawberries; a jug of cream.

And when the day was done I watched the
          sunset
  Like a cathedral window in the gloom,
With only music of the birds for vespers —
  And I was thankful for my country home.

Dorothy Wardell Boice, New York

All Serene

Clean hearth, a glowing fire, a sparkling
    windowpane;
Blast of wind in the tree-tops, a dash of
    beating rain;
Fresh-baked loaf, a pitcher of milk, a bowl
    on the table wait;
Children's heads at the window sill;
Father comes through the gate.

Nellie R. Nesselroade, West Virginia

Lines Upon Hearing a Political Convention on the Radio

Vain, boasting voices, empty as the autumn
    wind,
Have you forgotten? A people sit in
    need....
Solemn are the duties of a President.
He should not be some prating demagogue,
Nor chosen by a screaming, mad parade.
Alone within his chamber, alone with God,
Selected by a poll of all the people,
Bound by solemn oath and vow,
He should be as one anointed from on
    high....
Heavy is the price a nation pays for folly.
We can but pray to God,

Who hath never failed our land
A leader in its hour of trial.
But grim, grim is the rumbling of a people
    in their need,
And scattered as the dust before the wind
Shall be those who fail to heed.

Alice Fawley, West Virginia, 1932

XVI   *CONCERT*

Song

No toil so harsh but comes at length to rest,
No year so long but lilacs bloom again.
Earth turns no beaten wanderer from her breast,
But heals him with her sunshine and her rain.

Ben H. Smith, Illinois

TRAVEL NOTE: We drove up the west Mississippi shore out of Arkansas and crossed at Cape Girardeau into southern Illinois, which its natives call Egypt. It is a country of rough hills and narrowing, fertile valleys, fed by the River from the North. Ben Smith lives back from the River in that country, up between the wooded shoulders of rolling fields. Of his country he has written:

> God makes a rime
>   Of Egypt in the summertime:
> Wide fields of wheat
>   Arise to meet the sky.
>
> The pink, gay roses growing
>   Are proof that He is sowing
> A Heaven there whenever
>   June goes by.

We drove on the edge of Spring. Blooming Judas bushes, not roses, adorned those ridges; and they were wild and lovely. Asking our way, we went through Jonesboro, a sprawled hill town, one of the places where Lincoln and Douglas debated, and bearing about three miles south along a stream among the hills, found Ben Smith, packing strawberry plants in a place half cabin, half factory, on a little river-bottom. We knew him only by correspondence and he didn't know we were coming. 'Good Gosh!' he said, 'This is a pleasure!' A stockier, more rugged man than we had pictured him, he has the most melodious speaking voice we have heard for years.

He was packing Everbearing strawberry plants; it was really no time for a visit. The little we had time to say was confused and pleasant. The man who owned the farm joined us heartily in telling Ben to write more. 'The things he writes mean more to me than anything else I read,' said the Boss. 'I keep telling him to come up here to the office, any time he can, and use the typewriter. But I don't know what I'd do without him, if you Easterners take him over. He's the best man to handle men and plants I ever saw.' But the clock was ticking, and uprooted plants were waiting to go to new soil, before they wilted, through great distribution agencies. So we talked hurriedly. Ben had in his overalls pocket two lines he liked along with some he didn't. These were the two final lines in the brief song that adorns the head of these remarks. The other two lines we pieced out between us and agreed were just so-so. So here is a call for further help. If anyone who reads this can take pen in hand, and fit Ben's two last lines into a poem of anywhere from four to sixteen lines in length, we'll print it at the head of this Forum, and pay $20 for it.

[July, 1935]

HAVING READ 1108 manuscripts, and secured by mail Ben Smith's help in judging them, we announce a split decision and two $20 first awards, to Inez George Gridley and to E. H. Porter. There are at least ten other

poems we wish we could print, and the response as a whole
was of an extraordinary depth and reach. Some people
made around Ben's two lines a lament for the dead, some a
pagan sonnet, some a hymn. Some worked the lines into a
narrative; the prodigal's return. Some praised Earth's
generosity and slammed crop birth control. A few of the
poems from young people just out of school, without jobs,
and one or two from older Depression victims, were pitiful
beyond words. But the general tone was of robust rejoicing
in the earth's goodness and deep thankfulness for country
things...

[October, 1935]

XVII   *CLOSING CHORUS*

By Earth Restored

From grime and bitterness of city street
   I turn my feet to friendly country lane.
My head is humbled low with gray defeat.
   My heart is dully throbbing out its pain.
.... So tired! I lay me on the Earth's cool
      heart,
   Deep in the living grass I sink my face,
And for a soundless time I am a part
   Of her calm strength, her all-pervading
      grace.
My shameful bruises healed, my soul at rest,
   The will to live is strong in me again.
'Earth turns no beaten wanderer from her
      breast,
   But heals him with her sunshine and
      her rain.'

Inez George Gridley, New York State

Resurrection

In varied changelessness Earth waits serene,
   To summer's warmth there follows har-
      vesting,
And from her winter's workshop comes the
      clean
And tender resurrection of the spring.

Her wounded children turn from ways un-
blest,
And quarrels for joys of power and
empty gain;
'Earth turns no beaten wanderer from her
breast,
But heals him with her sunshine and
her rain.'

E. H. Porter, Maine

Healing Beauty

These are the things that bring a man
content:
Breath of green fields and cooling touch of
dew
After the hours of sunlit day are spent.
These are the things that bring him peace
anew:
Depths of great forests for his solitude,
Laughter of streams and blue-deep lakes
that lie
Half shadow-hidden in their quietude;
Far-reaching plains that meet an evening
sky.

'Earth turns no beaten wanderer from her
breast,
But heals him with her sunshine and her
rain.'
From her deep bosom he may rise refreshed

To meet the toil of daily life again;
For in Earth's healing beauty man will find
All things that bring tranquillity of mind.

Ethel B. Cheney, New Mexico

Earth Like a Mother

'Earth turns no beaten wanderer from her
    breast,
But heals him with her sunshine and her
    rain';
She spreads the purple clover for his rest,
And wakes him to a feast of golden grain.

The careless prodigal with lavish hand,
The frivolous who toss a coin in play,
When weary seek her unguent, cool and
    bland;
And like a mother, Earth turns none away.

Deep in her matrix lies the quickened seed,
Warmed into life. From earth the flowers
    spring:
White petals for the broken hearts that
    bleed,
And crimson for the lighter hearts that sing.

Earth offers solace; when in solemn mood,
Tired wanderers see the lengthening
    shadows creep,
And in the hush of night's long interlude,
She pillows every head in final sleep.

Ethel Johnston McNaught, Ohio

To Rise Again

We must not be afraid to walk apart
In strange new paths that texture an old hill,
To trade joy for an understanding heart,
To gain from soil a dignity of will!

We need to walk with dreams while dreams
     are bright
Like early sun or cadences of song;
To make the heavy climb before the light
Is hot with noon.

     When shadowed trees grow long
We seek a sheltered place to wait for rest —
Grown tired with labor, faint and weak with
     pain —
'Earth turns no beaten wanderer from her
     breast,
But heals him with her sunshine and her
     rain.'

Gertrude Scott Jewell, Ohio

Sonnet

See how your world of men can fail its sons!
Its wide-eyed blindness and deliberate
     greed; —
The steps that falter and the hearts that
     bleed;

While through its quickening torrent ever
    runs
The last despairing cry of luckless ones
Whose trust has failed them in their hour of
    need.
See those who serve the earth; — she takes
    their seed —
With rain and sun and wind her myrmi-
    dons, —
Changes and models to a perfect whole,
Seedling and child and fledgling in the nest,
And brings them back unto the seed
    again; —
Growth and completion as the seasons roll.
'Earth turns no beaten wanderer from her
    breast —
But heals him with her sunshine and her
    rain.'

Marjorie Goodburne, Michigan

Proof

Our faith in Nature's power is born anew
With every seed we to the Earth consign.
The miracle now hidden from our view
Tomorrow will have wrought a proof
    divine.

This thought sustains us as we long for rest
From striving false oases to attain.

'Earth turns no beaten wanderer from her
    breast
But heals him with her sunshine and her
    rain.'

Vera Willis-Reese, Illinois

I Know There Will Be Peace

I know there will be peace where silence is,
And joy where sunlight makes its shadow
    lace;
Remembered beauty waits where pools lie
    deep
And mountains lift their heads with solemn
    grace.
To these, the steps that strayed may come
    again,
And find release from cares, relief from
    pain —
'Earth turns no beaten wanderer from her
    breast,
But heals him with her sunshine and her
    rain.'

Carol Gridley, New York State

Forgotten Wounds

The hoofprint on the tender blade of grass,
The careless step that crushed the growing
    flower —

The torturers scarcely see them as they pass,
But Nature raises them with gentle power.

The scar upon the far-flung, rolling hills
Where hurried men once dragged the forest
     kings
Soon deepens to a creek that quickly fills
With sparkling water from long-hidden
     springs.

The soul of man yearning for long-sought
     rest,
The broken heart, the body racked with
     pain —
'Earth turns no beaten wanderer from her
     breast
But heals him with her sunshine and her
     rain.'

Helen Dykstra, Illinois

A Farmer Muses

I have watched the slow growth of tall
     trees
And I have seen the long speared light
Transfixing the shadows with flame
Or sere leaves transcending their boughs as
     dust
In earth's fermentation and patience;
And time, ruinous with each low wind's up-
     rising,

Unending, shaking out its locks, ravenous
    and bold.
And suddenly I am old with gray dust
But wise, foolishly, with bits of sterile clay.
I shall become a pilgrim of the light,
Foredoomed to sing with cymbal in the
    wind:
'Earth turns no beaten wanderer from her
    breast,
But heals him with her sunshine and her
    rain.'

Glenister Hoskins, Missouri